FAVORITE BRAND NAME
Mexican Fiesta!

Publications International, Ltd.

Favorite Brand Name Recipes at www.fbnr.com

Pictured on the front cover: Fiesta Beef Enchiladas *(page 148)*.
Pictured on the back cover *(clockwise from top):* Adobe Summer Salad *(page 76)*, Double Duty Tacos *(page 124)* and Fire and Ice *(page 346)*.

ISBN: 0-7853-8324-7

Library of Congress Control Number: 2002112006

Manufactured in China.

8 7 6 5 4 3 2 1

Microwave Cooking: Microwave ovens vary in wattage. Use the cooking times as guidelines and check for doneness before adding more time.

Preparation/Cooking Times: Preparation times are based on the approximate amount of time required to assemble the recipe before cooking, baking, chilling or serving. These times include preparation steps such as measuring, chopping and mixing. The fact that some preparations and cooking can be done simultaneously is taken into account. Preparation of optional ingredients and serving suggestions is not included.

Contents

p. 22

p. 140

p. 352

Introduction

Tacos, burritos, enchiladas—once considered exotic foods, they are now as familiar as earlier imports of pizza, quiche and egg rolls. Due to their vibrant flavors, enticing textural contrasts and eye-catching colors these Mexican dishes have been readily accepted into our menus.

Mexican cuisine is more diverse than the taco lover might suspect. Based on foods such as corn, tomatoes, chilies and beans, this cuisine has developed over centuries and was shaped by unique geography, climate, indigenous foods and the native Indian culture. Mexican cuisine was also enhanced, but not overshadowed, by the Spanish introduction of their cooking techniques and domestic animals.

The recipes in this book were chosen to illustrate the variety of this wonderful cuisine; they range from subtle to spicy, simple to complex, rustic to sophisticated. Using authentic ingredients and cooking techniques, these dishes are sure to be a success even for the novice cook.

MEXICAN COOKING TERMS

These ingredients are normally available in Mexican groceries. Many can be found in supermarkets and gourmet food stores and some can be purchased in other Latin American, Caribbean and even Oriental food stores.

Annatto Seeds (also called achiote): Small, hard crimson-colored seeds used primarily in the Mayan-based cooking of the Yucatan. The seeds impart a deep yellow color and mild but distinctive flavor. They are soaked to soften or ground to a fine powder before using.

Arroz: The Spanish word for "rice".

Burrito: A tortilla that is filled with a variety of choices, such as shredded or chopped meat, cheese and beans, then folded and rolled to enclose fillings.

Carnitas: Shredded pork that is cooked in small amounts of water and then finished in pork fat. It is usually used as a filling for tacos or burritos.

Chayote: A pear-shaped, pale green, soft-skinned squash with a delicious delicate flavor. It is also called mirliton or christophene. Chayote is generally available in the winter months and can be eaten raw, sautéed or baked. Store it in a plastic bag in the refrigerator for up to one month.

Chilies: See the descriptions on pages 6-7.

Chimichanga: Similar to a burrito, the chimichanga is enclosed with shredded meats, cheeses, rice and beans, then fried or deep-fried.

Chorizo: An orange- or red-colored, coarse-textured pork sausage sold bulk-style or stuffed into casings. The flavor ranges from highly seasoned to quite hot. Always remove the casing before using.

Cilantro (also called fresh coriander or Chinese parsley): A pungent herb with green delicate leaves, similar in appearance, but not flavor, to flat-leaf parsley. Used extensively in Mexican cooking, there is no substitute. Store it in the refrigerator for up to one week with the stems in a glass of water; cover the leaves with a plastic bag.

Empanada: A turnover made from a pastry crust and filled with a meat-and-vegetable filling. They range in size from those that serve several people to small, bite-size versions called empanaditas.

Enchilada: A tortilla with a meat or cheese filling rolled and topped with a salsa or sauce and cheese. They are traditionally baked before serving.

Fajitas: A tortilla typically topped with sliced grilled meat, bell peppers and onions, then rolled up wrap-style.

Jícama: A root vegetable with thin tan-brown skin and crisp, sweetish, white flesh. Shaped like a large turnip, jícama is most often used raw in salads or eaten as a refreshing snack. It should be peeled before using. Store it in the refrigerator for up to five days.

Masa Harina: A specially prepared flour used to make corn tortillas, tamales and other corn-based doughs. It is commonly available in 5-pound bags.

Mexican Chocolate: A mixture of chocolate, almonds, sugar and sometimes cinnamon and vanilla, ground together and formed into octagonal tablets. It is used in desserts, frothy chocolate beverages and, in small amounts, to add a subtle flavor enrichment to some mole sauces.

Mole: A traditional sauce that combines a blend of chilies, onions, garlic and Mexican chocolate. It may be red, green or yellow depending on the chilies used to make it.

Onions: White onions with a sharp bite are used in Mexican cooking and are necessary for flavor balance and authenticity. Yellow onions are too mild and impart an undesirable sweetness when cooked.

Pico de Gallo: A traditional salsa that consists of chopped fresh ingredients such as, oranges, jícama, bell peppers, onions, cucumbers and jalapeño peppers.

Pozole: A hearty, main-dish soup that includes a variety of ingredients including, pork or sometimes chicken, broth, garlic, hominy, cilantro and dried chiles. It may be topped with onions, cheese, chopped lettuce and radishes.

Quesadilla: A tortilla "sandwich" that includes many different filling combinations, such as meats, cheese, vegetables and beans. Quesadillas are heated under a broiler or fried and typically served as an appetizer.

Queso Chihuahua: A rich semi-soft cheese with a creamy color, mild flavor and good melting qualities. Mild Cheddar, Monterey Jack or Muenster can be used as substitutes.

Tomatillo (also called tomate verde or Mexican tomato): A small hard, green fruit with a papery outer husk that is pulled off before using. Tomatillos have a distinct acidic flavor and are used extensively in cooked sauces. They are available fresh or canned (often labeled tomatillo entero). There is no substitute.

Tamales: A dish in which corn flour (masa harina) is made into a dough and filled with savory fillings, such as shredded pork, beef, turkey or chicken, and then wrapped in a corn husk and steamed until it is cooked through. The husk is removed before serving.

Tex-Mex: A term used to describe dishes that have traits of foods from both Texas and Mexico. Examples are burritos, nachos and tacos.

Tortillas: The mainstay of Mexican cuisine. These thin, flat breads are made of corn or wheat flour. Nothing can compare with the taste and texture of freshly made tortillas, but making them at home (see recipes on pages 364 and 365) requires some practice and skill. Tortillas are readily available in the supermarket and these may be substituted for homemade tortillas. Corn tortillas usually measure between 5 and 6 inches in diameter; flour tortillas are available in many sizes, ranging from 7 to 12 inches in diameter.

Tostada: A fried tortilla topped with many ingredients, such as refried beans, shredded beef or chicken, tomatoes, lettuce, cheese, sour cream and guacamole.

CHILIES

The subject of chilies can be very confusing for beginning and experienced cooks alike. There are over 100 varieties of chilies in Mexico, each with its own unique characteristics. They are used both fresh and dried and either type can be whole or ground. The same chili can even be found under different names depending upon its region of origin. Chilies range in degree of heat from very mild to incendiary, and the heat can vary within a variety.

Due to increasing interest in Mexican foods, chilies that were once available only in Mexican grocery stores are now readily available in gourmet food stores and many local supermarkets. However, not all chilies will be available in all areas at all times. The following descriptions of the more common varieties will provide you with a basic knowledge of individual chili traits. With this knowledge, you can substitute one chili for another with similar traits. The character of the dish may change slightly, but it will still be delicious and enjoyable.

A Note of Caution: The heat of chilies comes from the seeds, the veins (the thin inner membranes to which the seeds are attached) and in the parts nearest the veins. For milder dishes, the veins and seeds are removed and discarded. The oils from the seeds and veins can be very irritating to the skin and can cause painful burning of the hands, eyes and lips. Do not touch your face while handling chilies and wash your hands well in warm soapy water after handling. Wear rubber gloves if your skin is especially sensitive or if you are handling a number of chilies.

Fresh Chilies

Fresh chilies will keep for several weeks refrigerated in a plastic bag lined with paper towels. (The towels absorb any moisture.) When purchasing fresh chilies, select those that have firm, unblemished skin.

Anaheim (also called California green chili): A light green chili that has a mild flavor with a slight bite. They are 4 to 6 inches long, about 1½ inches wide and have a rounded tip. Anaheims are also sold canned. For a spicier flavor, poblano chilies can be substituted.

Jalapeño: A small, dark green chili, normally 2 to 3 inches long and about ¾ inch wide with a blunt or slightly tapered end. Their flavor varies from hot to very hot. They are also sold canned and pickled. Serranos or any other small, hot, fresh chilies can be substituted.

Poblano: A very dark green, large triangular-shaped chili with a pointed end. Poblanos are usually 3½ to 5 inches long. Their flavor ranges from mild to quite hot. For a milder flavor, Anaheims can be substituted.

Serrano: A medium green, very small chili with a very hot flavor. It usually ranges from 1 to 1½ inches in length and is about ⅜ inch wide with a pointed end. Serranos are also available pickled. Jalapeños or any other small, hot, fresh chilies can be substituted.

Dried Chilies

Dried red (ripe) chilies are usually sold in cellophane packages of various weights. They will keep indefinitely if stored in a tightly covered container in a cool, dark, dry place.

Ancho: A fairly large, triangular-shaped chili, slightly smaller than the mulato chili. It has wrinkled, medium to dark reddish-brown skin. Anchos are full-flavored, ranging from mild to medium-hot.

Chipotle: A smoked and dried jalapeño chili. It has wrinkled, medium-brown skin and a rich, smoky, very hot flavor. Chipotles are also commonly available canned in adobo sauce.

De árbol: A very small, slender, almost needle-shaped chili with smooth, bright red skin and a very hot flavor.

Mulato: A triangular-shaped, large chili that has wrinkled, blackish-brown skin. Its flavor is rich, pungent and medium-hot.

Pasilla: A long, slender, medium-sized chili with wrinkled, blackish-brown skin. It has a pungent flavor, ranging from mild to quite hot. (Pasillas are sometimes labeled "negro chilies.")

Pequín (also spelled piquín): A very tiny chili shaped like an oval bead. It has a slightly wrinkled, orangish-red skin. Use pequín chilies with caution as their flavor is very, very hot. (These are sometimes labeled "tepin chilies.")

Appetizers

Fiesta Chicken Nachos

1 tablespoon BERTOLLI® Olive Oil
1 pound boneless, skinless chicken breasts
1 jar (16 ounces) RAGÚ® Cheese Creations!® Double Cheddar Sauce
1 bag (9 ounces) tortilla chips
2 green and/or red bell peppers, diced
1 small onion, chopped
1 large tomato, diced

In 12-inch skillet, heat oil over medium-high heat and cook chicken, stirring occasionally, 8 minutes or until no longer pink in center. Remove from skillet; cut into strips.

In same skillet, combine chicken and Ragú® Cheese Creations! Sauce; heat through.

On serving platter, arrange layer of tortilla chips, then ½ of the sauce mixture, bell peppers, onion and tomato; repeat, ending with tomato. Garnish, if desired, with chopped fresh cilantro and shredded lettuce. *Makes 4 servings*

Tip: For a spicier dish, add chopped jalapeño peppers or hot pepper sauce to suit your taste.

Fiesta Chicken Nachos

Chicken Empanadas

1 box (15 ounces) refrigerated pie crusts (two 11-inch crusts)
4 ounces cream cheese
2 tablespoons salsa
2 tablespoons chopped fresh cilantro
½ teaspoon ground cumin
½ teaspoon salt
¼ teaspoon garlic powder
1 cup finely chopped cooked chicken
1 egg, beaten
  Additional salsa

Remove pie crust pouches from box; let stand at room temperature 15 to 20 minutes.

Heat cream cheese in small heavy saucepan over low heat; cook and stir until melted. Add salsa, cilantro, cumin, salt and garlic powder; stir until smooth. Stir in chicken; remove from heat.

Unfold pie crusts; remove plastic film. Roll out slightly on lightly floured surface. Cut crusts into 3-inch rounds using biscuit cutter or drinking glass. Reroll pie crust scraps and cut enough additional to equal 20 rounds.

Preheat oven to 425°F. Place about 2 teaspoons chicken mixture in center of each round. Brush edges lightly with water. Pull one side of dough over filling to form half circle; pinch edges to seal.

Place 10 to 12 empanadas on foil-lined baking sheet; brush lightly with egg. Bake 16 to 18 minutes or until lightly brown. Serve with salsa. *Makes 10 appetizer servings*

Note: Empanadas can be prepared ahead of time and frozen. Simply wrap unbaked empanadas with plastic wrap and freeze. To bake, follow directions baking 18 to 20 minutes.

Chicken Empanadas

Black Bean Quesadillas

Nonstick cooking spray
4 (8-inch) flour tortillas
¾ cup (3 ounces) shredded reduced-fat Monterey Jack or Cheddar cheese
½ cup canned black beans, rinsed and drained
2 green onions with tops, sliced
¼ cup minced fresh cilantro
½ teaspoon ground cumin
½ cup salsa
2 tablespoons plus 2 teaspoons nonfat sour cream

1. Preheat oven to 450°F. Spray large nonstick baking sheet with cooking spray. Place 2 tortillas on prepared baking sheet; sprinkle each with half the cheese.

2. Combine beans, green onions, cilantro and cumin in small bowl; mix lightly. Spoon bean mixture evenly over cheese; top with remaining tortillas. Coat tops with cooking spray.

3. Bake 10 to 12 minutes or until cheese is melted and tortillas are lightly browned. Cut into quarters; top each tortilla wedge with 1 tablespoon salsa and 1 teaspoon sour cream. Transfer to serving plate.

Makes 8 servings

Velveeta® Bean Dip Olé

1 pound (16 ounces) VELVEETA® Pasteurized Prepared Cheese Product, cut up
1 can (16 ounces) refried beans
1 can (4 ounces) chopped green chilies

Microwave Velveeta, beans and chilies in 2-quart microwavable bowl on HIGH 8 to 9 minutes or until Velveeta is melted, stirring every 4 minutes. Serve hot with tortilla chips.

Makes 3 cups

Prep Time: 5 minutes
Microwave Time: 9 minutes

Black Bean Quesadillas

Classic Guacamole

4 tablespoons finely chopped white onion, divided
1 tablespoon plus 1½ teaspoons coarsely chopped fresh cilantro, divided
1 or 2 fresh serrano or jalapeño peppers,* seeded and finely chopped
¼ teaspoon chopped garlic (optional)
2 large soft avocados
1 medium tomato, peeled and chopped
1 to 2 teaspoons fresh lime juice
¼ teaspoon salt
Corn Tortilla Chips (recipe page 16) or packaged corn tortilla chips
Chilies and cilantro sprig for garnish

*Serrano and jalapeño peppers can sting and irritate the skin; wear rubber gloves when handling peppers and do not touch eyes. Wash hands after handling.

1. Combine 2 tablespoons onion, 1 tablespoon cilantro, peppers and garlic, if desired, in large mortar. Grind with pestle until almost smooth. (Mixture can be processed in blender, if necessary, but it will become more watery than desired.)

2. Cut avocados lengthwise into halves; remove and discard pits. Scoop out avocado flesh; place in bowl. Add pepper mixture. Mash roughly, leaving avocado slightly chunky.

3. Add tomato, lime juice, salt and remaining 2 tablespoons onion and 1½ teaspoons cilantro to avocado mixture; mix well. Serve immediately or cover and refrigerate up to 4 hours. Serve with Corn Tortilla Chips. Garnish, if desired. *Makes about 2 cups*

continued on page 16

Classic Guacamole

Corn Tortilla Chips

12 corn tortillas (6-inch diameter), day-old*
Vegetable oil
½ to 1 teaspoon salt

*If tortillas are fresh, let stand, uncovered, in single layer on wire rack 1 to 2 hours to dry slightly.

1. Stack 6 tortillas. Cutting through stack, cut tortillas into 6 or 8 equal wedges. Repeat with remaining tortillas.

2. Heat ½ inch oil in deep, heavy, large skillet over medium-high heat to 375°F; adjust heat to maintain temperature.

3. Fry tortilla wedges in single layer 1 minute or until crisp, turning occasionally. Remove and drain on paper towels. Repeat until all chips have been fried. Sprinkle chips with salt.

Makes 6 to 8 dozen chips

Layered Mexican Dip

1 package (8 ounces) cream cheese, softened
1 tablespoon plus 1 teaspoon taco seasoning mix
1 cup canned black beans
1 cup salsa
1 cup shredded lettuce
1 cup (4 ounces) shredded Cheddar cheese
½ cup chopped green onions
2 tablespoons sliced pitted ripe olives
Tortilla chips

Combine cream cheese and seasoning mix in small bowl. Spread on bottom of 9-inch pie plate.

Layer remaining ingredients over cream cheese mixture. Refrigerate until ready to serve. Serve with tortilla chips.

Makes 10 servings

Prep Time: 10 minutes plus refrigerating

Easy Sausage Empanadas

¼ **pound bulk pork sausage**
1 **(15-ounce) package refrigerated pie crusts (2 crusts)**
2 **tablespoons finely chopped onion**
⅛ **teaspoon garlic powder**
⅛ **teaspoon ground cumin**
⅛ **teaspoon dried oregano, crushed**
1 **tablespoon chopped pimiento-stuffed olives**
1 **tablespoon chopped raisins**
1 **egg, separated**

Let pie crusts stand at room temperature for 20 minutes or according to package directions. Crumble sausage into medium skillet. Add onion, garlic powder, cumin and oregano; cook over medium-high heat until sausage is no longer pink. Drain drippings. Stir in olives and raisins. Beat the egg yolk slightly; stir into sausage mixture, mixing well. Carefully unfold crusts. Cut into desired shapes using 3-inch cookie cutters. Place about 2 teaspoons of the sausage filling on half the cutouts. Top with remaining cutouts. Moisten fingers with water and pinch dough to seal edges. Slightly beat the egg white; gently brush over tops of empanadas. Bake in a 425°F oven 15 to 18 minutes or until golden brown.   *Makes 12 appetizer servings*

Prep Time: 25 minutes
Cook Time: 15 minutes

Favorite recipe from **National Pork Board**

Grilled Chicken Tostados

1 pound boneless skinless chicken breast halves
1 teaspoon ground cumin
¼ cup orange juice
¼ cup plus 2 tablespoons salsa, divided
1 tablespoon plus 2 teaspoons vegetable oil, divided
2 cloves garlic, minced
8 green onions
1 can (16 ounces) refried beans
4 (10-inch) *or* 8 (6- to 7-inch) flour tortillas
2 cups chopped romaine lettuce
1½ cups (6 ounces) shredded Monterey Jack cheese with jalapeño peppers
1 ripe medium avocado, diced (optional)
1 medium tomato, seeded and diced (optional)
Chopped fresh cilantro and sour cream (optional)

Place chicken in single layer in shallow glass dish; sprinkle with cumin. Combine orange juice, ¼ cup salsa, 1 tablespoon oil and garlic in small bowl; pour over chicken. Cover; marinate in refrigerator at least 2 hours or up to 8 hours, stirring mixture occasionally.

Prepare grill for direct cooking.

Drain chicken; reserve marinade. Brush green onions with remaining 2 teaspoons oil. Place chicken and green onions on grid. Grill, covered, over medium-high heat 5 minutes. Brush tops of chicken with half of reserved marinade; turn and brush with remaining marinade. Turn onions. Continue to grill, covered, 5 minutes or until chicken is no longer pink in center and onions are tender. (If onions are browning too quickly, remove before chicken is done.)

Meanwhile, combine beans and remaining 2 tablespoons salsa in small saucepan; cook, stirring occasionally, over medium heat until hot.

Place tortillas in single layer on grid. Grill, uncovered, 1 to 2 minutes per side or until golden brown. (If tortillas puff up, pierce with tip of knife or flatten by pressing with spatula.)

Transfer chicken and onions to cutting board. Slice chicken crosswise into ½-inch strips. Cut onions crosswise into 1-inch-long pieces. Spread tortillas with bean mixture; top with lettuce, chicken, onions, cheese, avocado and tomato, if desired. Sprinkle with cilantro and serve with sour cream, if desired. *Makes 4 servings*

Grilled Chicken Tostado

Chili con Queso

1 pound pasteurized process cheese spread, cut into cubes
1 can (10 ounces) diced tomatoes and green chilies, undrained
1 cup sliced green onions
2 teaspoons ground coriander
2 teaspoons ground cumin
¾ teaspoon hot pepper sauce
   Green onion strips (optional)
   Hot pepper slices (optional)

SLOW COOKER DIRECTIONS
Combine all ingredients except green onion strips and hot pepper slices in slow cooker until well blended. Cover and cook on LOW 2 to 3 hours or until hot.* Garnish with green onion strips and hot pepper slices, if desired.

Makes 3 cups

*Chili will be very hot; use caution when serving.

Señor Says: **Serve Chili con Queso with tortilla chips. Or, for something different, cut pita bread into triangles and toast in preheated 400°F oven for 5 minutes or until crisp.**

Chili con Queso

New-Age Quesadillas

8 whole wheat tortillas (7 inches)
2 cups (8 ounces) shredded Monterey Jack cheese with jalapeño peppers, divided
1 jar (7 ounces) roasted red peppers, drained and thinly sliced
1⅓ cups *French's®* French Fried Onions
Salsa (optional)

Place 4 tortillas on sheet of waxed paper. Sprinkle ¼ cup cheese over each tortilla. Arrange roasted peppers and French Fried Onions evenly over cheese. Sprinkle remaining cheese over onion layer. Top each layered tortilla with another tortilla, pressing down firmly.

Heat nonstick skillet over medium heat; spray with nonstick cooking spray. Using large spatula, place 1 quesadilla in skillet. Cook, pressing down with spatula, 2 to 3 minutes per side or until cheese melts and tortillas brown slightly. Repeat with remaining quesadillas.

To serve, cut each quesadilla into fourths. Serve with salsa, if desired.

Makes 4 to 6 appetizer servings

Prep Time: 20 minutes
Cook Time: 10 minutes

Nachos Supremos

½ of a 10-ounce bag tortilla chips
1 package (8 ounces) pasteurized process cheese with jalapeño peppers, cut into ½-inch cubes
1 cup (4 ounces) shredded Monterey Jack cheese
1⅓ cups *French's®* French Fried Onions
Chopped fresh tomatoes
Sliced ripe olives

Layer chips, cheeses and French Fried Onions on large microwavable dish. Microwave on HIGH 2 to 3 minutes or until cheeses melt. Top with tomatoes and olives. *Makes 4 servings*

Prep Time: 5 minutes
Cook Time: 2 minutes

New-Age Quesadillas

Beefy Nachos

1 pound ground beef
¼ cup chopped onion
⅓ cup A.1.® Steak Sauce
5 cups tortilla chips
1 cup (4 ounces) shredded Monterey Jack cheese
    Dairy sour cream (optional)
1 cup chopped tomato (optional)
¼ cup diced green chilies, drained (optional)
¼ cup sliced pitted ripe olives (optional)

In large skillet, over medium-high heat, brown beef and onion; drain. Stir in steak sauce. Arrange tortilla chips on large heatproof platter. Spoon beef mixture over chips; sprinkle with cheese. Broil, 6 inches from heat source, for 3 to 5 minutes or until cheese melts. Top with sour cream, tomato, chilies and olives, if desired. Serve immediately. *Makes 6 servings*

Microwave Directions: In 2-quart microwave-safe bowl, combine beef and onion; cover. Microwave at HIGH (100% power) for 5 to 6 minutes or until browned; drain. Stir in steak sauce. In 9-inch microwave-safe pie plate, layer half of each of the chips, beef mixture and cheese. Microwave at HIGH for 2 to 3 minutes or until heated through. Top with half of desired toppings. Repeat with remaining ingredients.

Ortega® Hot Poppers

1 can (4 ounces) ORTEGA® Whole Jalapeños, drained
1 cup (4 ounces) shredded mild Cheddar cheese
1 package (3 ounces) cream cheese, softened
¼ cup chopped fresh cilantro
½ cup all-purpose flour
2 eggs, lightly beaten
2 cups cornflakes cereal, crushed
   Vegetable oil
   ORTEGA® SALSA PRIMA™ Thick & Chunky
   Sour cream (optional)

CUT jalapeños lengthwise into halves; remove seeds.

BLEND Cheddar cheese, cream cheese and cilantro in small bowl. Place 1 to 1½ teaspoons cheese mixture into each jalapeño half; chill for 15 minutes or until cheese is firm.

DIP each jalapeño in flour; shake off excess. Dip in eggs; coat with cornflake crumbs.

ADD vegetable oil to 1-inch depth in medium skillet; heat over high heat for 1 minute. Fry jalapeños turning frequently with tongs, until golden brown on all sides. Remove from skillet; drain on paper towels. Serve with salsa and sour cream. *Makes 8 servings*

Pico de Gallo

1 small jicama, peeled
3 oranges
¼ cup lime juice
   Lime wedges for garnish
   Cilantro sprigs for garnish
   Salt
   Chili powder

Cut jicama into 3-inch matchsticks. Cut oranges in half lengthwise; cut halves crosswise into thin slices. Arrange jicama and oranges on serving plate; brush with lime juice. Garnish with lime wedges and cilantro. To serve, sprinkle with salt and chili powder to taste. *Makes 6 to 8 servings*

Cheesy Chorizo Wedges

Red & Green Salsa (recipe follows, optional)
8 ounces chorizo
1 cup (4 ounces) shredded mild Cheddar cheese
1 cup (4 ounces) shredded Monterey Jack cheese
3 flour tortillas (10-inch diameter)

1. Prepare Red & Green Salsa.

2. Remove and discard casing from chorizo. Heat medium skillet over high heat until hot. Reduce heat to medium. Crumble chorizo into skillet. Brown 6 to 8 minutes, stirring to separate meat. Remove with slotted spoon; drain on paper towels.

3. Preheat oven to 450°F. Combine cheeses in small bowl.

4. Place tortillas on baking sheets. Divide chorizo evenly among tortillas, leaving $1/2$ inch of edges of tortillas uncovered. Sprinkle cheese mixture over top.

5. Bake 8 to 10 minutes until edges are crisp and golden and cheese is bubbly and melted.

6. Transfer to serving plates; cut each tortilla into 6 wedges. Sprinkle Red & Green Salsa on wedges, if desired. *Makes 6 to 8 servings*

Red & Green Salsa

1 small red bell pepper
$1/4$ cup coarsely chopped fresh cilantro
3 green onions, cut into thin slices
2 fresh jalapeño peppers,* seeded and minced
2 tablespoons fresh lime juice
1 clove garlic, minced
$1/4$ teaspoon salt

*Jalapeño peppers can sting and irritate the skin; wear rubber gloves when handling peppers and do not touch eyes. Wash hands after handling.

1. Cut bell pepper lengthwise in half; remove and discard seeds and veins. Cut halves lengthwise into thin slivers; cut slivers crosswise into halves.

2. Mix all ingredients in small bowl. Let stand, covered, at room temperature 1 to 2 hours to blend flavors. *Makes 1 cup*

Cheesy Chorizo Wedges

Mexican Roll-Ups

> 6 uncooked lasagna noodles
> ¾ cup prepared guacamole
> ¾ cup chunky salsa
> ¾ cup (3 ounces) shredded nonfat Cheddar cheese
>   Additional salsa (optional)

1. Cook lasagna noodles according to package directions, omitting salt. Rinse with cool water; drain. Cool.

2. Spread 2 tablespoons guacamole onto each noodle; top each with 2 tablespoons salsa and 2 tablespoons cheese.

3. Roll up noodles jelly-roll fashion. Cut each roll-up in half to form two equal-size roll-ups. Serve immediately with salsa or cover with plastic wrap and refrigerate up to 3 hours.

Makes 12 appetizers

Mini Beef Tostadas

> 1 pound ground beef
> 1 tablespoon instant minced onion
> 1 can (8 ounces) refried beans
> 1 can (4 ounces) chopped green chilies, drained (optional)
> ½ cup bottled taco sauce
> 4 dozen round tortilla chips
> 1 cup (4 ounces) shredded Cheddar cheese

1. Preheat oven to 375°F. Cook and stir beef and onion in large skillet over medium heat about 10 minutes or until beef is no longer pink; drain and discard drippings.

2. Stir in beans, chilies, if desired, and taco sauce; cook and stir until bubbly, about 4 minutes. Spoon about 1 heaping tablespoon of the beef mixture on top of each tortilla chip; sprinkle with cheese. Place on baking sheets.

3. Bake until cheese is melted, about 2 minutes.

Makes 4 dozen

Mexican Roll-Ups

Velveeta® Salsa Dip

1 pound (16 ounces) VELVEETA® Pasteurized Prepared Cheese Product, cut up
1 cup TACO BELL® HOME ORIGINALS® Thick 'N Chunky Salsa

*TACO BELL and HOME ORIGINALS are registered trademarks owned and licensed by Taco Bell Corp.

Microwave Velveeta and salsa in 1½-quart microwavable bowl on HIGH 5 minutes or until Velveeta is melted, stirring after 3 minutes. Serve hot with tortilla chips or cut-up vegetables.   *Makes 3 cups*

Prep Time: 5 minutes
Microwave Time: 5 minutes

Jalapeño Kabobs Olé

1¼ cups A.1.® Original or A.1.® BOLD & SPICY Steak Sauce, divided
¼ cup finely chopped jalapeños (canned or fresh), mashed
1 (1-pound) beef top round steak, cut into ¾-inch cubes
18 cherry tomatoes, halved
18 fresh mushroom caps
2 small red onions, cut into wedges
1 cup dairy sour cream
¼ teaspoon chili powder

Blend 1 cup steak sauce and jalapeños in nonmetal bowl; add steak cubes, stirring to coat. Cover; refrigerate 1 hour, stirring occasionally.

Soak 18 (6-inch or 10-inch) wooden skewers in water at least 30 minutes.

Remove steak from marinade; discard marinade. Alternately thread each skewer with about 3 steak cubes, 2 tomato halves, 1 mushroom cap and 1 onion wedge. Grill kabobs over medium heat or broil 6 inches from heat source 4 to 6 minutes or until steak is desired doneness, turning occasionally.

Blend remaining ¼ cup steak sauce, sour cream and chili powder. Serve as dipping sauce with hot kabobs.

                                                                    Makes 18 appetizers

Velveeta® Salsa Dip

Tex-Mex Guacamole Platter

4 ripe avocados
¼ cup lime juice
3 large cloves garlic, crushed
2 tablespoons olive oil
½ teaspoon salt
¼ teaspoon black pepper
1 cup (4 ounces) shredded Colby-Jack cheese
1 cup seeded, diced plum tomatoes
⅓ cup sliced and pitted ripe olives
⅓ cup prepared salsa
1 tablespoon minced fresh cilantro
  Tortilla chips

Cut avocados in half, remove pits and scoop out flesh into food processor. Add lime juice, garlic, olive oil, salt and pepper. Process until almost smooth.

Spread avocado mixture evenly on large dinner plate or serving platter, leaving a border around edge. Top with cheese, tomatoes, olives, salsa and cilantro. Serve with chips.   *Makes 6 to 8 servings*

Señor Says: **If you buy an avocado that is not fully ripe, put it in a brown paper bag and keep it at room temperature. It will soften within a day or two. When you are ready to eat it, cut it with a stainless steel knife and sprinkle it with lemon or lime juice. This will prevent it from discoloring.**

Tex-Mex Guacamole Platter

Grilled Quesadilla Snacks

1½ cups (6 ounces) shredded Monterey Jack cheese
½ red or yellow bell pepper, chopped
2 ounces sliced smoked ham, cut into thin strips
2 ounces sliced smoked turkey, cut into thin strips
¼ cup finely chopped green onions
⅓ cup *French's*® Classic Yellow® Mustard
2 teaspoons ground cumin
10 flour tortillas (6 inch)

1. Combine cheese, bell pepper, ham, turkey and onions in medium bowl. Combine mustard and cumin in small bowl; mix well.

2. Place 5 tortillas on sheet of waxed paper. Spread 1 rounded teaspoon mustard mixture over each tortilla. Sprinkle cheese mixture evenly over mustard mixture. Top with another tortilla, pressing down firmly to form quesadilla.

3. Place quesadillas on oiled grid. Grill over medium heat 2 minutes or until cheese is melted and heated through, turning once. Cut each quesadilla into quarters. Serve with salsa and cilantro, if desired. *Makes 10 servings*

Prep Time: 30 minutes
Cook Time: 2 minutes

Mexican Chicken Rolls

>   6 boneless skinless chicken breasts halves (1½ pounds)
>   ¼ cup plus 1½ tablespoons plain dry bread crumbs, divided
>   1 teaspoon chili powder
>   ½ teaspoon ground cumin
>   ¾ cup (3 ounces) shredded Monterey Jack cheese
>   2 tablespoons chopped pimientos, drained
>   1 green onion, chopped
>   3 tablespoons *Frank's® RedHot®* Cayenne Pepper Sauce, divided
>   1½ tablespoons grated Parmesan cheese
>   ½ teaspoon paprika
>   2 tablespoons butter, melted
>   Salsa (optional)

1. Pound chicken breasts between 2 sheets of plastic wrap to ¼-inch thickness. Set aside. Combine ¼ cup bread crumbs, chili powder and cumin in medium bowl. Stir in Monterey Jack cheese, pimientos, onion and 2 tablespoons **Frank's RedHot** Sauce; mix well.

2. Preheat oven to 400°F. Spoon about 2 tablespoons filling down center of each chicken breast half, leaving 1-inch border along edges. Fold edges over filling; place, seam side down, in greased 2-quart baking dish.

3. Combine remaining 1½ tablespoons bread crumbs, Parmesan cheese and paprika in small bowl; set aside. Mix butter and remaining 1 tablespoon **Frank's RedHot** Sauce in another small bowl; brush over stuffed chicken breasts. Sprinkle bread crumb mixture over chicken breasts. Bake 30 minutes or until chicken is no longer pink. Serve with salsa, if desired.   *Makes 6 servings*

Prep Time: 20 minutes
Cook Time: 30 minutes

Tortilla Pizzettes

1 cup chunky salsa
1 cup refried beans
2 tablespoons chopped fresh cilantro
½ teaspoon ground cumin
3 large (10-inch) flour tortillas
1 cup (4 ounces) shredded Mexican cheese blend

Pour salsa into strainer; let drain at least 20 minutes.

Meanwhile, combine refried beans, cilantro and cumin in small bowl; mix well. Preheat oven to 400°F. Spray baking sheet lightly with nonstick cooking spray; set aside.

Cut each tortilla into 2½-inch circles with round cookie cutter (9 to 10 circles per tortilla). Spread each tortilla circle with refried bean mixture, leaving ¼ inch around edge. Top each with heaping teaspoon drained salsa; sprinkle with about 1 teaspoon cheese.

Place pizzettes on prepared baking sheet. Bake about 7 minutes or until tortillas are golden brown.

Makes about 30 pizzettes

Señor Says: **You can make your own Mexican cheese blend as well. Try combining a ½ cup each of Cheddar and Monterey Jack cheeses. Add, if desired, ¼ teaspoon chili powder for some spice.**

Tortilla Pizzettes

Taco Chicken Nachos

2 small boneless skinless chicken breasts (about 8 ounces)
1 tablespoon plus 1½ teaspoons taco seasoning mix
1 teaspoon olive oil
¾ cup nonfat sour cream
1 can (4 ounces) chopped mild green chilies, drained
¼ cup minced red onion
1 bag (8 ounces) baked nonfat tortilla chips
1 cup (4 ounces) shredded reduced-fat Cheddar or Monterey Jack cheese
½ cup chopped tomato
¼ cup pitted ripe olive slices (optional)
2 tablespoons chopped fresh cilantro (optional)

1. Bring 2 cups water to a boil in small saucepan. Add chicken. Reduce heat to low; cover. Simmer 10 minutes or until chicken is no longer pink in center. Remove from saucepan; cool. Chop chicken.

2. Combine taco seasoning mix and oil in small bowl; mix until smooth paste forms. Stir in sour cream. Add chicken, green chilies and onion; mix lightly.

3. Preheat broiler. Arrange tortilla chips on small ovenproof plates or large platter; cover chips with chicken mixture and cheese. Broil, 4 inches from heat, 2 to 3 minutes or until chicken mixture is hot and cheese is melted. Sprinkle evenly with tomato, olives and cilantro, if desired. Serve hot.

Makes 12 servings

Taco Chicken Nachos

Miniature Quesadillas

¼ **teaspoon chili powder**
¼ **teaspoon ground cumin**
¼ **teaspoon salt**
¼ **teaspoon dried oregano leaves**
1 **cup shredded Cheddar cheese**
½ **cup shredded Monterey Jack cheese (about 2 ounces)**
1½ **teaspoons CRISCO® Oil**
4 **(6-to 7-inch) flour tortillas**
Fresh salsa (optional)

1. Combine chili powder, cumin, salt and oregano in large plastic food storage bag. Add Cheddar and Monterey Jack cheese. Shake to coat cheese.

2. Heat 1½ teaspoons Crisco® Oil in medium skillet. Fry one tortilla on medium-high heat 30 seconds or until golden brown. Turn, fry 30 seconds longer. Repeat with remaining tortillas.

3. Place fried tortillas on baking sheet. Sprinkle with cheese mixture. Broil 3 inches from heat 1½ to 2½ minutes, or until cheese melts. Cut each quesadilla into 4 pieces. Top with salsa, if desired. Serve hot.

Makes 4 servings

Preparation Time: about 5 to 10 minutes
Total Time: 20 minutes

Miniature Quesadillas

Soups & Salads

Chilled Fire Gazpacho

1½ **cups tomato juice**
⅓ **cup extra-virgin olive oil**
¼ **cup fresh lime juice**
6 **medium ripe tomatoes, coarsely chopped (about 5 cups)**
1 **medium cucumber, coarsely chopped**
1 **red bell pepper, coarsely chopped**
2 **large green onions, coarsely chopped**
2 **tablespoons chopped fresh parsley**
2 **teaspoons TABASCO® brand Pepper Sauce**
½ **teaspoon salt**

Combine tomato juice, olive oil and lime juice in medium bowl. Purée tomatoes, cucumber, red bell pepper and green onions in small batches in food processor or blender, adding tomato juice mixture gradually. (Do not purée completely; soup should retain some crunch.) Stir in parsley, TABASCO® Sauce and salt. Chill until ready to serve.

To serve, ladle gazpacho into chilled soup bowls or mugs. Serve with additional TABASCO® Sauce and garnish with avocado slices, if desired. *Makes 6 servings*

Chilled Fire Gazpacho

Velveeta® Spicy Southwest Corn Cheese Soup

1 package (10 ounces) frozen sweet corn, thawed, drained
1 clove garlic, minced
1 tablespoon butter or margarine
¾ pound (12 ounces) VELVEETA® Pasteurized Prepared Cheese Product, cut up
1 can (4 ounces) chopped green chilies
¾ cup chicken broth
¾ cup milk
2 tablespoons chopped fresh cilantro

1. Cook and stir corn and garlic in butter in large saucepan on medium-high heat until tender. Reduce heat to medium.

2. Stir in remaining ingredients; cook until Velveeta is melted and soup is thoroughly heated. Top each serving with crushed tortilla chips, if desired.   *Makes 4 (1-cup) servings*

Prep Time: 15 minutes
Cook Time: 10 minutes

Mexicali Vegetable Soup

½ pound ground beef
½ cup chopped onion
3½ cups (two 15-ounce cans) beef broth
1¾ cups (14½-ounce can) small white beans, drained
1 cup (1 large) sliced zucchini
1 cup frozen sliced carrots
1 package (1¼ ounces) ORTEGA® Taco Seasoning Mix

COOK beef and onion in large saucepan until beef is browned; drain. Add broth, beans, zucchini, carrots and seasoning mix. Bring to a boil. Reduce heat to low; cook, covered, for 15 to 20 minutes.

Makes 6 to 8 servings

Velveeta® Spicy Southwest
Corn Cheese Soup

Pozole

1 large onion, thinly sliced
1 tablespoon olive oil
2 teaspoons dried oregano leaves
1 clove garlic, minced
½ teaspoon ground cumin
2 cans (about 14 ounces each) chicken broth
1 package (10 ounces) frozen corn
1 to 2 cans (4 ounces each) chopped green chilies, undrained
1 can (2¼ ounces) sliced ripe olives, drained
¾ pound boneless skinless chicken breasts

1. Combine onion, oil, oregano, garlic and cumin in Dutch oven. Cover and cook over medium heat about 6 minutes or until onion is tender, stirring occasionally.

2. Stir broth, corn, chilies and olives into onion mixture. Cover and bring to a boil over high heat.

3. While soup is cooking, cut chicken into thin strips. Add to soup. Reduce heat to medium-low; cover and cook 3 to 4 minutes or until chicken is no longer pink.   *Makes 6 servings*

Hint: For a special touch, sprinkle Pozole with chopped fresh cilantro before serving.

Prep and Cook Time: 20 minutes

Señor Says: **A Dutch oven is a large pot or kettle with a tight-fitting lid that prevents steam from escaping while cooking. It is used for the slow, moist cooking of a large quantity of food. It is ideal for soups and stews and for braising large pieces of meat.**

Pozole

Corn & Red Pepper Soup

2 tablespoons butter or margarine
2 cups seeded and coarsely chopped red bell peppers
1 medium onion, thinly sliced
1 can (about 14 ounces) chicken broth
1 package (10 ounces) frozen whole kernel corn*
½ teaspoon ground cumin
½ cup sour cream
   Salt
   White pepper
   Sunflower seeds for garnish

*Cut raw kernels from 4 large ears of yellow or white corn to substitute for frozen corn.

Melt butter in 3-quart saucepan over medium heat. Add bell peppers and onion; cook until tender. Add chicken broth, corn and cumin.

Bring to a boil over high heat. Reduce heat to low. Cover and simmer 20 minutes or until corn is tender.

Pour into blender or food processor container; process until smooth. **Pour into sieve set over bowl; press mixture with rubber spatula to extract all liquid. Discard pulp. Return liquid to pan; whisk in sour cream until evenly blended. Add salt and white pepper to taste. Reheat but do not boil. Serve in individual bowls. Garnish with sunflower seeds.

Makes 4 servings

**Omit straining, if desired. Return processed soup to pan; whisk in sour cream. Proceed as above.

Albondigas

1 pound lean ground beef
½ small onion, finely chopped
1 egg
¼ cup dry bread crumbs
1 tablespoon chili powder
1 teaspoon ground cumin
½ teaspoon salt
3 cans (about 14 ounces each) chicken broth
1 medium carrot, thinly sliced
1 package (10 ounces) frozen corn
1 package (10 ounces) thawed frozen leaf spinach
¼ cup dry sherry

1. Mix ground beef, onion, egg, bread crumbs, chili powder, cumin and salt in medium bowl until well blended. Place mixture on lightly oiled cutting board; pat evenly into 1-inch-thick square. Cut into 36 squares with sharp knife; shape each square into a ball.

2. Place meatballs slightly apart in single layer in microwavable container. Cover and cook at HIGH (100%) 3 minutes or until meatballs are no longer pink (or just barely pink) in center.

3. While meatballs are cooking, bring broth and carrot to a boil in covered Dutch oven over high heat. Stir in corn and sherry. Transfer meatballs to broth with slotted spoon. Reduce heat to medium and simmer 3 to 4 minutes or until meatballs are cooked through. Add to soup and simmer until heated through.   *Makes 6 servings*

Note: For a special touch, sprinkle soup with chopped fresh cilantro.

Prep and Cook Time: 30 minutes

Mexican Tortilla Soup

6 to 8 corn tortillas (6-inch diameter), preferably day-old
2 large, very ripe tomatoes, peeled, seeded (about 1 pound)
⅔ cup coarsely chopped white onion
1 large clove garlic
   Vegetable oil
7 cups chicken broth
4 sprigs fresh cilantro
3 sprigs fresh mint (optional)
½ to 1 teaspoon salt
4 or 5 dried pasilla chilies
5 ounces queso Chihuahua or Monterey Jack cheese, cut into ½-inch cubes
¼ cup coarsely chopped fresh cilantro

1. Stack tortillas; cutting through stack, cut tortillas into ½-inch-wide strips. Let strips stand, uncovered, on wire rack 1 to 2 hours to dry slightly.

2. Place tomatoes, onion and garlic in blender; process until smooth. Heat 3 tablespoons oil in saucepan over medium heat until hot. Add tomato mixture. Cook 10 minutes, stirring frequently.

3. Add broth and cilantro sprigs to saucepan; bring to a boil over high heat. Reduce heat to low. Simmer, uncovered, 20 minutes. Add mint, if desired, and salt; simmer 10 minutes more. Remove and discard cilantro and mint. Keep soup warm.

4. Heat ½ inch oil in deep, heavy, large skillet over medium-high heat to 375°F; adjust heat to maintain temperature.

5. Fry half of tortilla strips at a time, in single layer, 1 minute or until crisp, turning strips occasionally. Remove with slotted spoon; drain on paper towels.

6. Fry chilies in same oil about 30 seconds or until puffed and crisp, turning chilies occasionally. Do not burn chilies. Drain on paper towels. Cool slightly; crumble coarsely.

7. Ladle soup into bowls. Let each person add chilies, tortilla strips, cheese and chopped cilantro according to taste.

Makes 4 to 6 servings

Mexican Tortilla Soup

Taco Soup

Nonstick cooking spray
½ pound ground sirloin or ground round beef
1 cup chopped onion
1 can (16 ounces) pinto beans in Mexican-style sauce
1 can (about 14 ounces) no-salt-added stewed tomatoes, undrained
1 can (10 ounces) diced tomatoes and green chilies
2 teaspoons chili powder
5 (8-inch) corn tortillas
5 cups shredded iceberg lettuce
½ cup shredded low-sodium, reduced-fat sharp Cheddar cheese
¼ cup chopped fresh cilantro (optional)

1. Preheat oven to 350°F. Spray large saucepan with cooking spray. Heat over medium-high heat until hot. Add beef and onion. Cook and stir 6 minutes or until beef is browned. Add beans, stewed tomatoes with juice, diced tomatoes and green chilies and chili powder. Bring to a boil. Reduce heat to low. Cover and simmer 10 minutes.

2. Place tortillas on baking sheet. Spray tortillas lightly on both sides with cooking spray. Using pizza cutter, cut each tortilla into 6 wedges. Bake 5 minutes.

3. Divide lettuce equally among soup bowls. Ladle beef mixture over lettuce. Top with cheese and cilantro, if desired. Serve with tortilla wedges. *Makes 5 servings*

Prep and Cook Time: 25 minutes

Chilled Avocado Soup

3 small onion slices, each ¼ inch thick, divided
1 can (14½ ounces) chicken broth
½ cup plain yogurt
1½ tablespoons lemon juice
1 large ripe avocado, halved and pitted
3 to 5 drops hot pepper sauce
Salt
White pepper
¼ cup finely chopped tomato
¼ cup finely chopped cucumber
Cilantro sprigs for garnish

Place 1 onion slice, chicken broth, yogurt and lemon juice in blender or food processor container fitted with metal blade; process until well blended. Remove pulp from avocado; spoon into blender. Process until smooth. Pour into medium container with tight-fitting lid. Add hot pepper sauce and salt and pepper to taste. Finely chop the remaining 2 onion slices; add to soup. Stir in tomato and cucumber. Cover and refrigerate 2 hours or up to 24 hours. Serve cold in individual bowls. Garnish with cilantro and additional chopped tomato and cucumber, if desired.   *Makes 6 servings*

Gazpacho

1½ pounds fresh tomatoes, seeded and chopped
1½ cups tomato juice
1 medium cucumber, peeled, seeded and chopped
¼ cup finely chopped green bell pepper
¼ cup finely chopped onion
2 tablespoons olive or vegetable oil
2 tablespoons white wine vinegar
1½ teaspoons LAWRY'S® Garlic Salt
¼ teaspoon dried oregano, crushed
LAWRY'S® Seasoned Pepper

In large bowl, combine all ingredients except Seasoned Pepper; mix well. Refrigerate until chilled. Add a sprinkle of Seasoned Pepper to each serving.

Makes 5 to 6 servings

Serving Suggestion: Serve in individual chilled bowls.

Hint: For more spice, stir in ¼ teaspoon hot pepper sauce before chilling.

Mexican Hot Pot

1 tablespoon canola oil
1 onion, sliced
3 cloves garlic, minced
2 teaspoons red pepper flakes
2 teaspoons dried oregano leaves, crushed
1 teaspoon ground cumin
1 can (28 ounces) tomatoes, chopped
2 cups whole kernel corn, fresh or frozen
1 can (15 ounces) chick-peas, rinsed and drained
1 can (15 ounces) pinto beans, rinsed and drained
1 cup water
6 cups shredded iceberg lettuce

1. Heat oil in stockpot or Dutch oven over medium-high heat. Add onion and garlic; cook and stir 5 minutes. Add red pepper flakes, oregano and cumin; mix well.

2. Stir in tomatoes, corn, chick-peas, pinto beans and water; bring to a boil over high heat.

3. Reduce heat to medium-low; cover and simmer 15 minutes. Top individual servings with 1 cup shredded lettuce. Serve hot.

Makes 6 servings

Chicken Tortilla Soup

2 large ripe avocados, halved and pitted
4 teaspoons TABASCO® brand Green Pepper Sauce, divided
½ teaspoon salt *or* to taste
3 (14½-ounce) cans chicken broth
3 boneless, skinless chicken breast halves (about 1 pound)
2 tablespoons uncooked rice
1 large tomato, seeded and chopped
½ cup chopped onion
¼ cup finely chopped cilantro
   Tortilla chips
½ cup (2 ounces) shredded Monterey Jack cheese

Scoop out avocado into medium bowl and mash with fork. Add 1½ teaspoons TABASCO® Green Pepper Sauce and salt; blend gently but thoroughly. Set aside.

Heat chicken broth to boiling in 4-quart saucepan. Add chicken breast halves; reduce heat and cook until chicken is opaque. Remove chicken and cut into bite-size pieces. Add rice and cook about 15 minutes or until tender. Return chicken to saucepan. Just before serving, stir in tomato, onion, cilantro and remaining 2½ teaspoons TABASCO® Green Pepper Sauce.

To serve, break small handful of tortilla chips into bottom of each bowl. Ladle soup over tortilla chips. Top with cheese and 1 rounded tablespoon avocado mixture. Serve immediately with additional TABASCO® Green Pepper Sauce, if desired.   *Makes 8 servings*

Chicken Tortilla Soup

Southwest Corn and Turkey Soup

3 dried ancho chilies (each about 4 inches long) *or* 6 dried New Mexico chilies (each about 6 inches long)

2 small zucchini

1 medium onion, thinly sliced

3 cloves garlic, minced

1 teaspoon ground cumin

3 cans (about 14 ounces each) fat-free reduced-sodium chicken broth

1½ to 2 cups (8 to 12 ounces) shredded cooked dark turkey meat

1 can (15 ounces) chick-peas or black beans, rinsed and drained

1 package (10 ounces) frozen corn

¼ cup cornmeal

1 teaspoon dried oregano leaves

⅓ cup chopped fresh cilantro

1. Cut stems from chilies; shake out seeds. Place chilies in medium bowl; cover with boiling water. Let stand 20 to 40 minutes or until chilies are soft; drain. Cut open lengthwise and lay flat on work surface. With edge of small knife, scrape chili pulp from skin (thicker-skinned ancho chilies will yield more flesh than thinner-skinned New Mexico chilies). Finely mince pulp; set aside.

2. Cut zucchini in half lengthwise; slice crosswise into ½-inch-wide pieces. Set aside.

3. Spray large saucepan with cooking spray; heat over medium heat. Add onion; cook, covered, 3 to 4 minutes or until light golden brown, stirring several times. Add garlic and cumin; cook and stir about 30 seconds or until fragrant. Add chicken broth, reserved chili pulp, zucchini, turkey, chick-peas, corn, cornmeal and oregano; bring to a boil over high heat. Reduce heat to low; simmer 15 minutes or until zucchini is tender. Stir in cilantro; ladle into bowls and serve.

Makes 6 servings

Southwest Corn and Turkey Soup

Picante Black Bean Soup

4 slices bacon
1 large onion, chopped
1 clove garlic, minced
2 cans (15 ounces each) black beans, undrained
1 can (about 14 ounces) beef broth
1¼ cups water
¾ cup picante sauce
½ to 1 teaspoon salt
½ teaspoon dried oregano leaves
Sour cream
Crackers and additional picante sauce for serving

1. Using scissors, cut through several slices of bacon at once, cutting into ½×½-inch pieces.

2. Cook and stir bacon in large saucepan over medium-high heat until crisp. Remove with slotted spoon; drain on paper towels.

3. Add onion and garlic to drippings in saucepan; cook and stir 3 minutes.

4. Add beans with liquid, broth, water, ¾ cup picante sauce, salt to taste and oregano. Reduce heat to low. Simmer, covered, 20 minutes.

5. Ladle into soup bowls; dollop with sour cream. Sprinkle with bacon. Serve with crackers and additional picante sauce. *Makes 6 to 8 servings*

Picante Black Bean Soup

Fajita Steak Salad

¾ cup A.1.® THICK & HEARTY Steak Sauce
½ cup mild thick and chunky salsa
3 tablespoons vegetable oil, divided
2 tablespoons red wine vinegar
2 cups thinly sliced red, yellow and/or green bell peppers
1 cup thin onion wedges
2 cloves garlic, minced
1 pound cooked steak, cut into julienne strips (about 2 cups)
4 cups torn mixed salad greens
1 cup shredded Cheddar cheese (4 ounces)
½ cup sliced pitted ripe olives
   Tortilla chips

In small bowl, blend steak sauce, salsa, 2 tablespoons oil and vinegar; set aside.

In large skillet, over medium-high heat, sauté peppers, onion and garlic in remaining 1 tablespoon oil until tender. In large nonmetal bowl, combine pepper mixture, steak and steak sauce mixture. Cover; refrigerate until serving time.

To serve, toss chilled steak mixture with salad greens, cheese and olives. Serve with tortilla chips.

Makes 6 servings

Fajita Steak Salad

Soups & Salads 63

Avocados with Tomato Relish

1 tablespoon cider vinegar
1 tablespoon fresh orange juice
1 teaspoon grated orange peel
¼ teaspoon salt
    Dash black pepper
3 tablespoons olive oil
3 fresh plum tomatoes (about ½ pound)
¼ cup coarsely chopped fresh cilantro
2 tablespoons finely chopped mild red onion
1 fresh jalapeño pepper,* seeded and finely chopped
2 large, firm ripe avocados
2 cups shredded iceberg lettuce
    Cilantro sprig, orange peel and tomato slice for garnish

*Jalapeño peppers can sting and irritate the skin; wear rubber gloves when handling peppers and do not touch eyes. Wash hands after handling.

1. Mix vinegar, orange juice, orange peel, salt and black pepper in medium bowl. Gradually add oil, whisking continuously, until dressing is thoroughly blended.

2. Add tomatoes, chopped cilantro, onion and jalapeño pepper to dressing; toss lightly to mix. Let stand, covered, at room temperature up to 2 hours to blend flavors.

3. Just before serving, cut avocados lengthwise into halves; remove and discard pits. Pare avocados and cut lengthwise into ½-inch-thick slices.

4. Arrange avocados over lettuce-lined plates; top with tomato relish. Garnish, if desired.

Makes 4 servings

Avocados with Tomato Relish

Soups & Salads   65

Outrageous Mexican Chicken Salad

6 cups shredded lettuce
1 bag (9 ounces) tortilla chips, crushed (about 3 cups)
2 cups cubed cooked chicken
1 can (15½ ounces) kidney beans, rinsed and drained
1½ cups prepared HIDDEN VALLEY® The Original Ranch® Salad Dressing
½ cup (2 ounces) shredded Cheddar cheese
Tomatoes and olives

Combine lettuce, tortilla chips, chicken, beans, dressing and cheese in a large bowl. Garnish with tomatoes and olives.

Makes 4 to 6 servings

Black Bean Mexicali Salad

1 can (15 ounces) black beans, rinsed and drained
6 ounces roasted red bell peppers, cut in thin strips or coarsely chopped
½ cup chopped red or yellow onion, divided
⅓ cup mild chipotle or regular salsa
2 tablespoons cider vinegar
2 ounces mozzarella cheese, cut in ¼-inch cubes

Place all ingredients except 1 tablespoon of the onion and the cheese in medium mixing bowl. Toss gently to blend well. Let stand 15 minutes to absorb flavors. Just before serving, gently fold in all but 2 tablespoons of cheese. Sprinkle remaining cheese and onion on top.

Makes 7 servings

Note: Serve within 30 minutes to take advantage of flavors at their peak.

Fiesta Salad

4 cups shredded lettuce

1½ cups cubed pared jicama

1 cup tomato wedges

1 can (4 ounces) diced green chile peppers

⅓ cup thinly sliced green onions with tops

1½ cups (6 ounces) shredded Cheddar cheese

1 package (1 ounce) **HIDDEN VALLEY® The Original Ranch®** Seasoning & Salad Dressing Mix

2 cups (1 pint) sour cream

1 tablespoon lime juice

1 teaspoon chili powder

1 tablespoon taco sauce

1 ripe avocado, sliced

2 cups coarsely crushed tortilla chips

Line salad bowl with shredded lettuce. Fill center with jicama, tomatoes, chile peppers, green onions and cheese. Cover and refrigerate. Meanwhile, whisk together salad dressing mix, sour cream, lime juice, chili powder and taco sauce until smooth; refrigerate. Just before serving, arrange avocado slices on top and sprinkle with crushed tortilla chips. Toss with 1 cup (or more, if desired) prepared dressing and serve.

Makes 4 to 6 servings

Mexican Pork Salad

1 pound boneless pork loin, cut into 3×½×¼-inch strips
4 cups shredded lettuce
1 medium orange, peeled, sliced and quartered
1 medium avocado, peeled, seeded and diced
1 small red onion, sliced and separated into rings
1 tablespoon vegetable oil
1 teaspoon chili powder
¾ teaspoon salt
½ teaspoon dried oregano leaves, crushed
¼ teaspoon ground cumin

Place lettuce on serving platter. Arrange orange, avocado and red onion over lettuce. Heat oil in large skillet; add chili powder, salt, oregano and cumin. Add pork loin strips and stir-fry over medium-high heat 5 to 7 minutes or until pork is tender. Spoon hot pork strips over lettuce mixture. Serve immediately.

Makes 4 servings

Favorite recipe from **National Pork Board**

Mexican Pork Salad

Gazpacho Salad

1½ cups peeled and coarsely chopped tomatoes*
1 cup peeled, seeded and diced cucumber
¾ cup chopped onion
½ cup chopped red bell pepper
½ cup fresh or frozen corn kernels, cooked and drained
1 tablespoon lime juice
1 tablespoon red wine vinegar
2 teaspoons water
1 teaspoon extra-virgin olive oil
1 teaspoon minced fresh garlic
¼ teaspoon salt
¼ teaspoon black pepper
Pinch ground red pepper
1 medium head romaine lettuce, torn into bite-sized pieces
1 cup peeled and diced jicama
½ cup fresh cilantro sprigs

*To peel tomatoes easily, blanch in boiling water 30 seconds; immediately transfer to bowl of cold water, then peel.

1. Combine tomatoes, cucumber, onion, bell pepper and corn in large bowl. Combine lime juice, vinegar, water, oil, garlic, salt, black pepper and ground red pepper in small bowl; whisk until well blended. Pour over tomato mixture; toss well. Cover and refrigerate several hours to allow flavors to blend.

2. Toss together lettuce, jicama and cilantro in another large bowl. Divide lettuce mixture evenly among 6 plates. Place ⅔ cup chilled tomato mixture on top of lettuce, spreading to edges.

Makes 6 servings

Gazpacho Salad

Marinated Vegetable Salad

¾ cup **ORTEGA®** Salsa Prima-Thick & Chunky Mild
¼ cup (about 2 limes) lime juice
¼ cup chopped fresh parsley or cilantro *or* 2 teaspoons dried parsley
2 tablespoons olive oil
2 cups (2 medium) chopped tomatoes
1¾ cups (15-ounce can) kidney beans, rinsed, drained
1 cup (1 medium) ripe avocado, peeled, seeded and chopped
1 cup (1 medium) chopped zucchini
½ cup (4-ounce can) **ORTEGA®** Diced Green Chiles
Lettuce leaves (optional)

COMBINE salsa, lime juice, parsley and oil in large bowl. Add tomatoes, kidney beans, avocado, zucchini and chiles. Toss to coat well. Cover; refrigerate for at least 2 hours. Serve over lettuce.

Makes 6 to 8 servings

Jicama Slaw

2 to 3 large oranges
½ cup minced red onion
½ cup lightly packed fresh cilantro, coarsely chopped plus additional cilantro for garnish
⅓ cup reduced-fat mayonnaise
2 tablespoons frozen orange juice concentrate, thawed
1 tablespoon sugar
1 jalapeño or serrano pepper,* seeded and minced
4 cups shredded jicama**
3 cups shredded green cabbage

*Jalapeño and serrano peppers can sting and irritate the skin; wear rubber gloves when handling peppers and do not touch eyes. Wash hands after handling peppers.

**Peel jicama with sharp knife, removing brown outer skin and thin coarse layer of flesh underneath. Shred jicama in food processor.

1. Grate orange peel with grater or zester; measure 1 tablespoon. Cut away remaining white pith from oranges, working over small bowl to collect juices. Cut between membranes to separate orange segments; set segments aside. Squeeze membranes with hand to remove more juice.

2. Combine onion, cilantro, mayonnaise, orange juice concentrate, sugar, jalapeño pepper, orange peel and juice from orange in large bowl.

3. Add jicama and cabbage; stir to combine. Reserve several orange segments for garnish; cut remaining segments in half and stir into slaw. Transfer slaw to serving bowl and garnish with orange peel and cilantro.

Makes 6 servings

Mexican Salad

1 cup uncooked pinto beans
½ pound BOB EVANS® Original Recipe or Zesty Hot Roll Sausage
¾ cup mayonnaise
3 tablespoons chili powder
2½ tablespoons ground cumin
1 teaspoon salt
1 head iceberg lettuce
1 (9-ounce) bag nacho cheese tortilla chips, broken into pieces
1 cup (4 ounces) shredded sharp Cheddar cheese

Rinse beans and place in 2-quart saucepan. Add 1 quart water; bring to a boil. Cover and simmer 50 minutes or until beans are tender. Drain, rinse and refrigerate beans. Crumble and cook sausage in medium saucepan until browned; drain well on paper towels. Chop sausage finely and refrigerate. Combine mayonnaise, chili powder, cumin and salt in small bowl; mix well. Refrigerate at least 30 minutes. Rinse, chop and dry lettuce. Place lettuce in large salad bowl and refrigerate until ready to assemble salad.

To assemble, toss lettuce with beans, mayonnaise mixture and tortilla chips. Spoon into salad bowls or plates; sprinkle with sausage and cheese. Refrigerate leftovers.

Makes 6 to 8 servings

Grilled Chicken Taco Salad

1 can (14½ ounces) DEL MONTE® Diced Tomatoes with Garlic & Onion
⅓ cup thick and chunky salsa, hot or medium
2 tablespoons vegetable oil
2 tablespoons red wine vinegar or cider vinegar
1 large head romaine lettuce, chopped (10 to 12 cups)
4 boneless, skinless chicken breast halves, grilled and cut bite size*
1 can (8 ounces) kidney beans, drained (optional)
1 cup (4 ounces) shredded sharp Cheddar cheese
3 cups broken tortilla chips

*Or, substitute 3 cups cubed cooked chicken.

1. Drain tomatoes, reserving 1 tablespoon liquid. Chop tomatoes; set aside.

2. Make dressing in small bowl by blending reserved tomato liquid, salsa, oil and vinegar.

3. Toss lettuce with tomatoes, chicken, beans, if desired, and cheese in large bowl. Add dressing as desired. Add chips; toss. Season with salt and pepper, if desired. Serve immediately. Garnish, if desired.

Makes 4 servings

Prep Time: 15 minutes

Señor Says: **To add variety to the salad, add chopped avocado, sliced green onions, olives, corn, sliced radishes and chopped cilantro, as desired.**

Grilled Chicken Taco Salad

Adobe Summer Salad

3 cups cooked converted white rice, chilled
1 can (about 15 ounces) black beans, rinsed and drained
2 cups diced red and/or yellow or orange bell peppers
1 large tomato, chopped
1 cup diced jicama
1 cup diced cooked chicken or turkey breast
¾ cup sliced green onions
¼ cup chopped fresh cilantro
1 cup thick and chunky salsa
2 tablespoons fresh lime juice
2 tablespoons vegetable oil
¼ teaspoon salt
8 large romaine lettuce leaves
    Lime wedges (optional)

1. Combine rice, beans, bell peppers, tomato, jicama, chicken, green onions and cilantro in large bowl; mix well.

2. Combine salsa, lime juice, oil and salt in small bowl. Add to salad; toss well. (Salad may be served immediately or covered and chilled up to 8 hours before serving.) Serve salad over lettuce leaves with lime wedges.

Makes 6 servings

Señor Says: **Converted rice is the unhulled grain that is soaked, processed by steam pressure and dried before milling. The result is a rice kernel that is more nutritious and less starchy than polished white rice. It takes longer to cook than white rice and absorbs more liquid during cooking. Converted rice tends to be less sticky and fluffy.**

Adobe Summer Salad

Zesty Taco Salad

2 tablespoons vegetable oil
1 clove garlic, finely chopped
¾ pound ground turkey
1¾ teaspoons chili powder
¼ teaspoon ground cumin
3 cups washed and torn lettuce leaves
1 can (14½ ounces) Mexican-style diced tomatoes, drained
1 cup rinsed and drained canned chick-peas or pinto beans
⅔ cup chopped peeled cucumber
⅓ cup frozen corn, thawed
¼ cup chopped red onion
1 to 2 jalapeño peppers,* seeded and finely chopped (optional)
1 tablespoon red wine vinegar
12 nonfat tortilla chips
Fresh greens (optional)
Fresh cilantro (optional)

*Jalapeño peppers can sting and irritate the skin. Wear rubber gloves when handling peppers and do not touch eyes. Wash hands after handling.

1. Combine oil and garlic in small bowl; let stand 1 hour at room temperature.

2. Combine turkey, chili powder and cumin in large nonstick skillet. Cook over medium heat 5 minutes or until turkey is no longer pink, stirring to crumble.

3. Combine turkey, lettuce, tomatoes, chick-peas, cucumber, corn, onion and jalapeño pepper, if desired, in large bowl. Remove garlic from oil; discard garlic. Add vinegar to oil. Drizzle over salad; toss to coat. Serve on tortilla chips and fresh greens, if desired. Serve with additional tortilla chips and garnish with cilantro, if desired. *Makes 4 servings*

Zesty Taco Salad

Poultry

Chicken Fajita Wraps

1 pound chicken tenders
¼ cup lime juice
4 cloves garlic, minced, divided
Nonstick cooking spray
1 red bell pepper, sliced
1 green bell pepper, sliced
1 yellow bell pepper, sliced
1 large red onion, cut into ¼-inch slices
½ teaspoon ground cumin
¼ teaspoon salt
¼ teaspoon ground red pepper
8 (8-inch) flour tortillas, warmed
Salsa

1. Combine chicken, lime juice and 2 cloves garlic in medium bowl; toss to coat. Cover and marinate 30 minutes in refrigerator, stirring occasionally.

2. Spray large nonstick skillet with cooking spray; heat over medium heat until hot. Add chicken mixture; cook and stir 5 to 7 minutes or until chicken is browned and no longer pink in center. Remove chicken from skillet. Drain excess liquid from skillet, if necessary.

3. Add bell peppers, onion and remaining 2 cloves garlic to skillet; cook and stir about 5 minutes or until vegetables are tender. Sprinkle with cumin, salt and red pepper. Return chicken to skillet; cook and stir 1 to 2 minutes.

4. Fill tortillas with chicken mixture. Serve with salsa. Garnish, if desired. *Makes 4 servings*

Chicken Fajita Wraps

Southwest Chicken and Beans

3 tablespoons lemon juice

2 tablespoons seasoned stir-fry or hot oil*, divided

2 tablespoons finely chopped onion

1 tablespoon white wine vinegar

1 clove garlic, minced

2 teaspoons chili powder

1 teaspoon salt

½ teaspoon dried oregano leaves

½ teaspoon ground cumin

½ teaspoon black pepper

1 pound boneless skinless chicken breasts or tenders, cut into ¼-inch strips

1 medium red onion, cut into thin strips

2 large red bell peppers, cut into ¼-inch strips

1 tablespoon minced cilantro

2 cans (16 ounces each) refried beans, warmed

Tortilla chips, salsa and sour cream

*Seasoned stir-fry oils differ in "heat". If oil is extremely peppery, use 1 tablespoon vegetable oil and 1 tablespoon hot oil.

1. Combine lemon juice, 1 tablespoon oil, chopped onion, vinegar, garlic, chili powder, salt, oregano, cumin and black pepper in medium bowl. Add chicken; toss to coat well. Cover and refrigerate 45 minutes to 8 hours.

2. Heat remaining 1 tablespoon oil in wok or large skillet over high heat. Add chicken mixture; stir-fry 3 minutes. Add onion strips; stir-fry 4 minutes. Add bell peppers; stir-fry 2 to 3 minutes or until vegetables are crisp-tender. Sprinkle with cilantro.

3. Serve chicken and vegetable mixture over beans with tortilla chips, salsa and sour cream on the side.

Makes 4 to 5 servings

Southwest Chicken and Beans

Barbecued Chicken with Chili-Orange Glaze

1 to 2 dried de arbol chilies*
1½ teaspoons grated orange peel
½ cup fresh orange juice
2 tablespoons tequila
2 cloves garlic, minced
¼ teaspoon salt
¼ cup vegetable oil
1 broiler-fryer chicken (about 3 pounds), cut into quarters
Orange slices (optional)
Cilantro sprigs (optional)

*For milder flavor, discard seeds from chili peppers. Since chili peppers can sting and irritate the skin, wear rubber gloves when handling peppers and do not touch eyes. Wash hands after handling chili peppers.

Crush chilies into coarse flakes in mortar with pestle. Combine chilies, orange peel, orange juice, tequila, garlic and salt in small bowl. Gradually add oil, whisking continuously, until marinade is thoroughly blended.

Arrange chicken in single layer in shallow glass baking dish. Pour marinade over chicken; turn pieces to coat. Marinate, covered, in refrigerator 2 to 3 hours, turning chicken over and basting with marinade several times.

Prepare charcoal grill for direct cooking or preheat broiler. Drain chicken, reserving marinade. Bring marinade to a boil in small saucepan over high heat. Grill chicken on covered grill or broil, 6 to 8 inches from heat, 15 minutes, brushing frequently with marinade. Turn chicken over. Grill or broil 15 minutes more or until chicken is no longer pink in center and juices run clear, brushing frequently with marinade.* Garnish with orange slices and cilantro, if desired. *Makes 4 servings*

*Do not baste during last 5 minutes of grilling.

*Barbecued Chicken
with Chili-Orange Glaze*

Chicken & Chili Chimichangas

2 boneless skinless chicken breast halves (5 ounces each)
½ teaspoon ground cumin
1 cup (4 ounces) shredded reduced-fat Monterey Jack cheese
1 can (4 ounces) diced mild green chilies
6 (7-inch) flour tortillas
Green Onion-Cilantro Sauce (recipe follows)

1. Preheat oven to 400°F. Bring 4 cups water to a boil in large saucepan over high heat. Add chicken, cover and remove from heat. Let stand 15 minutes or until chicken is no longer pink in center. Drain; let cool slightly. Tear into small pieces. Place in medium bowl and sprinkle with cumin. Add cheese and chilies; stir to combine.

2. Spoon about ½ cup chicken mixture down center of each tortilla. Fold bottom of tortilla up over filling, then fold sides over filling. Brush each chimichanga lightly with water, coating all around. Place on baking sheet, about 1 inch apart. Bake 12 to 15 minutes or until tortillas are crisp and just barely golden. Top with Green Onion-Cilantro Sauce. Serve with shredded romaine lettuce and tomato slices, if desired.

Makes 6 servings

Green Onion-Cilantro Sauce

¼ cup plain nonfat yogurt
¼ cup low-fat sour cream
⅓ cup chopped green onions
⅓ cup lightly packed fresh cilantro

Combine all ingredients in food processor or blender; process until smooth.

Makes about 1 cup sauce

Chicken Mariachis with Pineapple Salsa

1 can (8 ounces) crushed pineapple, packed in juice, undrained
⅓ cup CRISCO® Oil*
¼ cup lime juice or lemon juice
2 tablespoons finely chopped cilantro
1 tablespoon chili powder
1 teaspoon garlic salt
1 teaspoon onion powder
8 chicken drumsticks
1 cup prepared fresh tomato salsa
CRISCO® Butter Flavor No-Stick Cooking Spray

*Use your favorite Crisco Oil product.

Drain juice from pineapple into shallow glass dish. Reserve pineapple. Add oil, lime juice, cilantro, chili powder, garlic salt and onion powder to juice. Whisk to blend.

Rinse chicken; pat dry. Add to juice mixture, turning to coat. Cover. Refrigerate several hours or overnight.

Combine salsa and reserved pineapple. Cover. Refrigerate.

Heat broiler or grill.

Spray broiler pan or grill rack with Crisco Spray. Broil or grill chicken about 10 to 12 minutes per side or until chicken is no longer pink in center. Serve with salsa mixture. *Makes 4 to 8 servings*

Arroz con Pollo Burritos

2½ cups shredded cooked chicken
1 package (1.0 ounce) LAWRY'S® Taco Spices & Seasonings
3¼ cups water, divided
2 tablespoons vegetable oil
1 cup long-grain rice
1 can (8 ounces) tomato sauce
1 teaspoon LAWRY'S® Lemon Pepper
1 large tomato, chopped
¼ cup chopped green onions
8 medium flour tortillas, warmed
Shredded cheddar cheese

In large deep skillet, combine chicken, Taco Spices & Seasonings and ¾ cup water. Bring to a boil over medium-high heat; reduce heat to low and simmer, uncovered, 10 minutes. Remove and set aside. In same skillet, heat oil. Add rice and cook over medium-high heat until golden. Add remaining 2½ cups water, tomato sauce and Lemon Pepper. Bring to a boil over medium-high heat; reduce heat to low, cover and simmer 20 minutes. Stir in chicken mixture, tomato and green onions; mix well. Heat 5 minutes. Place a heaping ½ cup filling on each tortilla. Fold in sides and roll to enclose filling. Place filled burritos seamside down on baking sheet. Sprinkle with cheese. Heat in 350°F oven 5 minutes to melt cheese.

Makes 8 servings

Señor Says: **The literal translation of Arroz con Pollo is rice with chicken. For extraordinary Arroz con Pollo burritos, garnish with salsa and guacamole.**

Arroz con Pollo Burritos

Soft Tacos with Chicken

8 (6- or 7-inch) corn tortillas
2 tablespoons butter or margarine
1 medium onion, chopped
1½ cups shredded cooked chicken
1 can (4 ounces) diced green chilies, drained
2 tablespoons chopped fresh cilantro
1 cup (½ pint) sour cream
Salt
Black pepper
1½ cups (6 ounces) shredded Monterey Jack cheese
1 large avocado, peeled, pitted and diced
Green taco sauce

Stack and wrap tortillas in foil. Warm in 350°F oven 15 minutes or until heated through. Melt butter in large skillet over medium heat. Add onion; cook until tender. Add chicken, green chilies and cilantro. Cook 3 minutes or until mixture is hot. Reduce heat to low. Stir in sour cream; add salt and pepper to taste. Heat gently; do not boil. To assemble each taco, spoon about 3 tablespoons chicken mixture into center of each tortilla; sprinkle with 2 tablespoons cheese. Top with avocado; drizzle with 1 to 2 teaspoons taco sauce. Sprinkle tacos with remaining cheese. Roll tortilla into cone shape or fold in half to eat.

Makes 8 tacos

Soft Taco with Chicken

Green Enchiladas with Chicken

1 pound fresh tomatillos *or* 2 cans (13 ounces each) tomatillos, drained
1 can (7 ounces) diced green chilies, undrained
2 tablespoons vegetable oil
1 medium onion, finely chopped
1 clove garlic, minced
1 can (about 14 ounces) chicken broth
Vegetable oil for frying
12 (6- or 7-inch) corn tortillas
3 cups shredded cooked chicken
2½ cups (10 ounces) shredded Monterey Jack cheese
1 cup (½ pint) sour cream
4 green onions with tops, thinly sliced
Cilantro sprigs for garnish

Preheat oven to 350°F. If using fresh tomatillos, remove husks; wash thoroughly. Place tomatillos in 2-quart pan; add ½ inch water. Bring to a boil. Cover; reduce heat and simmer 10 minutes or until tender. Drain. Place tomatillos and chilies in blender or food processor container fitted with metal blade; process until puréed. Heat the 2 tablespoons oil in large skillet over medium heat. Add onion and garlic; cook until onion is tender. Stir in purée and chicken broth. Simmer, uncovered, until sauce has reduced to about 2½ cups and is consistency of canned tomato sauce.

Heat ½ inch oil in 7- to 8-inch skillet over medium-high heat. Place 1 tortilla in hot oil; cook 2 seconds on each side or just until limp. Drain briefly on paper towels, then dip softened tortilla into tomatillo sauce. Transfer sauced tortilla to a plate. Place about ¼ cup of the chicken and 2 tablespoons of the cheese across center of tortilla; roll to enclose. Place enchilada, seam side down, in 15×10-inch baking pan. Repeat until all tortillas are filled. Spoon remaining sauce over enchiladas, making sure all ends are moistened; reserve remaining cheese. Cover. Bake 20 to 30 minutes or until hot in center. Uncover and top with reserved cheese. Continue baking, uncovered, 10 minutes or until cheese is melted. Spoon sour cream down center of enchiladas; sprinkle with green onions. Garnish with cilantro.

Makes 6 servings

Grilled Fajitas

1 package (about 1 pound) PERDUE® Fresh Seasoned, Boneless Fajita Chicken Thighs
4 tablespoons canola oil, divided
1½ tablespoons lime juice
1½ teaspoons fajita seasoning or chili powder
2 bell peppers (1 red, 1 green), seeded and sliced into strips
1 onion, sliced into rings
8 to 12 flour tortillas (8-inch size)
Guaca-Salsa (recipe follows)

Prepare grill for cooking. Brush thighs lightly with 1 tablespoon oil. Grill 6 to 8 inches over medium-hot coals 16 to 20 minutes, turning 2 to 3 times during cooking.

Meanwhile, in mixing bowl, combine remaining 3 tablespoons oil, lime juice and fajita seasoning. Toss peppers and onion rings with mixture. Place vegetables in grill basket or on sheet of heavy-duty aluminum foil; grill vegetables alongside chicken.

Wrap tortillas in foil packet and warm on grill during last 5 to 10 minutes of cooking time. Remove thighs from grill and thinly slice. Wrap chicken, peppers and onion rings in warm tortillas. Add a dollop of Guaca-Salsa to each fajita.

Makes 4 to 6 servings

Guaca-Salsa: In small bowl, combine 2 mashed avocados with ½ cup sour cream, ¼ cup prepared salsa and 2 teaspoons lime juice. Serve with fajitas.

Mexican Lasagna

4 boneless skinless chicken breast halves
2 tablespoons vegetable oil
2 teaspoons chili powder
1 teaspoon ground cumin
1 can (14½ ounces) diced tomatoes with garlic, drained
1 can (8 ounces) tomato sauce
1 teaspoon hot pepper sauce (optional)
12 (6-inch) corn tortillas
1 cup part-skim ricotta cheese
1 can (4 ounces) diced green chilies
¼ cup chopped fresh cilantro, divided
1 cup (4 ounces) shredded Cheddar cheese

Preheat oven to 375°F. Cut chicken into ½-inch pieces.

Heat oil in large skillet over medium heat. Add chicken, chili powder and cumin. Cook 4 minutes or until tender, stirring occasionally. Stir in diced tomatoes, tomato sauce and hot pepper sauce, if desired; bring to a boil. Reduce heat; simmer 2 minutes.

Combine ricotta cheese, chilies and 2 tablespoons cilantro in small bowl; mix until well blended.

Spoon half of chicken mixture into 12×8-inch baking dish. Top with 6 tortillas, ricotta cheese mixture, remaining 6 tortillas, remaining chicken mixture, Cheddar cheese and remaining 2 tablespoons cilantro. Bake 25 minutes or until heated through.
Makes 6 to 8 servings

Mexican Lasagna

Velveeta® Tex-Mex Chicken & Rice

4 small boneless skinless chicken breast halves (about 1 pound)
1 can (15 ounces) pinto beans, drained *or* **1½ cups cooked pinto beans**
1 can (14½ ounces) chicken broth
1 cup TACO BELL® HOME ORIGINALS®* Thick 'N Chunky Salsa
2 cups MINUTE® White Rice, uncooked
½ pound (8 ounces) VELVEETA® Pasteurized Prepared Cheese Product, cut up

*TACO BELL and HOME ORIGINALS are registered trademarks owned and licensed by Taco Bell Corp.

1. Spray large skillet with no stick cooking spray. Add chicken; cover. Cook on medium-high heat 4 minutes on each side or until cooked through. Remove chicken from skillet.

2. Add beans, broth and salsa to skillet; stir. Bring to boil.

3. Stir in rice and Velveeta. Top with chicken; cover. Cook on low heat 5 minutes. Sprinkle with chopped cilantro, if desired, before serving.

Makes 4 servings

Prep Time: 5 minutes
Cook Time: 15 minutes

Velveeta® Tex-Mex
Chicken & Rice

Chicken Mole

3 small dried pasilla chilies, toasted, seeded, deveined and rinsed
3 small dried mulato chilies, toasted, seeded, deveined and rinsed
1½ cups boiling water
¼ cup sesame seeds
3 whole cloves
1 piece cinnamon stick (about 1 inch)
¼ teaspoon whole coriander seeds
⅛ teaspoon whole anise seeds
¼ cup vegetable oil
¼ cup whole unblanched almonds
¼ cup raisins
6 whole chicken legs, thighs attached (about 3 pounds)
¼ teaspoon salt
½ cup coarsely chopped white onion
2 cloves garlic
1 tablespoon tomato paste
1½ ounces Mexican chocolate, coarsely chopped
1 cup chicken broth
Tomato wedges and cilantro sprigs for garnish
Green Rice Pilaf (recipe page 312, optional)

1. Place pasilla and mulato chilies in medium bowl; cover with boiling water. Let stand 1 hour.

2. Toast sesame seeds in dry, heavy skillet over medium heat 2 minutes or until golden, stirring frequently. Remove from skillet. Combine cloves, cinnamon stick, coriander seeds and anise seeds in skillet; toast over medium heat 20 to 30 seconds until they start to change color and become fragrant, stirring frequently. Remove from skillet.

3. Heat oil in 12-inch skillet over medium heat until hot. Add almonds. Cook and stir 2 to 3 minutes until brown. Remove with slotted spoon; drain on paper towels. Add raisins. Cook and stir 30 seconds or until puffed. Remove with slotted spoon.

4. Sprinkle chicken with salt. Cook in same skillet over medium heat 10 minutes or until browned, turning once. Remove to plate. Remove all but 2 tablespoons oil from skillet.

5. Place raisins in blender; process until finely ground. Coarsely chop almonds; add to blender. Process until finely ground. Add onion and garlic to blender; process until finely ground.

6. Process 2 tablespoons sesame seeds with on/off pulses in electric spice grinder to fine powder. Add to blender. Process clove mixture in grinder to fine powder; add to blender.

7. Add chilies, $1/3$ cup of the soaking water and the tomato paste to blender; process until smooth. If mixture is too thick, add just enough of the remaining soaking water, 1 teaspoon at a time, until blender blade can spin. Discard remaining soaking water.

8. Reheat oil in skillet over medium heat until hot. Reduce heat to medium-low. Add chili mixture. Cook and stir 5 minutes. Add chocolate; cook and stir 2 minutes or until melted. Gradually stir in broth. Cook and stir 5 minutes.

9. Return chicken to skillet. Reduce heat to low. Cover and simmer 45 minutes or until chicken is tender and juices run clear, turning chicken occasionally. Sprinkle remaining sesame seeds over chicken just before serving. Garnish, if desired. Serve with Green Rice Pilaf, if desired.

Makes 6 servings

Chicken Tostadas

> 3 cups shredded cooked chicken
> 1½ cups TACO BELL® HOME ORIGINALS®* Thick 'N Chunky Salsa
> 8 tostada shells
> 1 tub (8 ounces) PHILADELPHIA® Light Cream Cheese Spread
> 1½ cups shredded lettuce
> 1 tomato, chopped
> 1 package (8 ounces) KRAFT® 2% Milk Shredded Reduced Fat Mild Cheddar Cheese
>
> *TACO BELL and HOME ORIGINALS are registered trademarks owned and licensed by Taco Bell Corp.

TOSS chicken with salsa.

SPREAD tostada shells with cream cheese spread; top with chicken mixture, lettuce, tomatoes and cheese. Serve with additional salsa and jalapeño pepper slices, if desired.   *Makes 8 servings*

Prep Time: 20 minutes

Santa Fe Skillet Chili

Nonstick cooking spray
1 to 1¼ pounds ground turkey (93% lean)
1 cup chopped onion
1 teaspoon bottled minced garlic
1 tablespoon chili powder
1 tablespoon ground cumin
¼ to ½ teaspoon ground red pepper
1 can (15½ ounces) chili beans in spicy sauce, undrained
1 can (14½ ounces) Mexican- or chili-style stewed or diced tomatoes, undrained
1 can (4 ounces) chopped green chilies, undrained

1. Spray large deep skillet with cooking spray. Cook turkey, onion and garlic over medium-high heat, breaking meat apart with wooden spoon.

2. Sprinkle chili powder, cumin and red pepper evenly over turkey mixture; cook and stir 3 minutes or until turkey is no longer pink.

3. Stir in beans with sauce, tomatoes with juice and chilies with liquid. Reduce heat to medium; cover and simmer 10 minutes, stirring occasionally. Ladle chili into bowls.   *Makes 4 servings*

Prep and Cook Time: 19 minutes

 Señor Says: **Offer a variety of toppings with this skillet chili, such as chopped fresh cilantro, sour cream, shredded Cheddar or Monterey Jack cheese and diced ripe avocado. Serve with warm corn tortillas or corn bread.**

Santa Fe Skillet Chili

Turkey and Roasted Pepper Quesadillas

Nonstick cooking spray
8 (6-inch) corn tortillas
1 jar (7¼ ounces) roasted red peppers, drained and diced
4 ounces diced cooked turkey breast
1 cup (4 ounces) shredded part-skim mozzarella cheese
½ cup chopped fresh cilantro
½ cup salsa (optional)

1. Spray small nonstick skillet with cooking spray; heat over medium heat until hot. Brush 1 tortilla lightly on both sides with water. Heat in skillet 1 minute on each side or until hot.

2. Layer ¼ of the diced peppers, turkey, cheese and cilantro on tortilla. Top with second tortilla; press lightly. Brush top of tortilla with water. Turn quesadilla to heat second side. Cook 3 minutes or until ingredients are heated through. Remove from heat. Repeat with remaining tortillas.

3. Cut quesadillas into halves. Serve with salsa, if desired. *Makes 4 servings*

Señor Says: **Make your own roasted bell peppers. To roast bell peppers, preheat oven to 425°F. Cut 2 medium peppers in half; remove stems, seeds and membranes. Place peppers, cut sides down, on prepared baking sheet. Bake 20 to 25 minutes or until skins are browned, turning occasionally. Transfer peppers from baking sheet to paper bag; close bag tightly. Let stand 10 minutes or until peppers are cool enough to handle and skins are loosened. Peel off skins using sharp knife; discard skins. Cut peppers into strips.**

Turkey and Roasted Pepper Quesadillas

Mexican Turkey Tenderloin with Chunky Tomato Sauce

1 teaspoon ground cumin

¾ teaspoon garlic powder

1 pound turkey breast tenderloin, cut into 4 pieces

2 tablespoons vinegar

2 teaspoons sugar

2 teaspoons cornstarch

1 cup coarsely chopped tomatoes

1 cup chopped zucchini

⅓ cup chopped onion

1 tablespoon chopped fresh cilantro *or* 1 teaspoon dried cilantro leaves, crushed

1 tablespoon chopped jalapeño pepper*

*Jalapeño peppers can sting and irritate the skin; wear rubber gloves when handling peppers and do not touch eyes. Wash hands after handling peppers.

Preheat broiler. Combine cumin and garlic powder in small bowl; rub mixture on both sides of turkey. Place turkey on broiler pan. Broil 4 inches below heat 5 minutes. Turn and broil about 5 minutes more or until juices run clear and turkey is no longer pink in center.

Meanwhile, combine vinegar, sugar and cornstarch in small saucepan until smooth. Stir in tomatoes, zucchini, onion, cilantro and jalapeño pepper. Cook and stir over medium heat until mixture boils and thickens. Cook and stir 2 minutes more. Spoon over turkey.   *Makes 4 servings*

Oven-Roasted Turkey Breast Fajitas

2 teaspoons vegetable oil
1 medium onion, sliced
1 cup green or red bell pepper strips (or combination)
4 kosher flour tortillas (6 or 7 inches), warmed
12 ounces HEBREW NATIONAL® Sliced Oven Roasted Turkey Breast
8 thin slices ripe avocado
¾ cup prepared salsa

Heat oil in small nonstick skillet over medium heat. Add onion and pepper strips; cook until tender. Fill each tortilla with 3 ounces turkey breast, ½ cup onion mixture, 2 slices avocado and 3 tablespoons salsa. Roll up tortilla; serve immediately.   *Makes 4 servings*

Burrito Turkey Burgers

Vegetable cooking spray
2 pounds ground turkey
1 cup chopped onion
1 can (4 ounces) chopped green chilies, drained
1 package (1¼ ounces) taco seasoning mix
8 (8-inch) flour tortillas
1 can (16 ounces) nonfat refried beans
Shredded lettuce
½ cup shredded nonfat Cheddar cheese, divided
Salsa (optional)

1. Spray cold grill rack with vegetable cooking spray. Preheat charcoal grill for direct-heat cooking.

2. In medium bowl combine turkey, onion, chilies and seasoning mix. Shape turkey mixture into 8 (9×2-inch) rectangular-shaped burgers. Grill burgers 3 to 4 minutes; turn and continue cooking 2 to 3 minutes or until 160°F is reached on meat thermometer and meat is no longer pink in center.

3. Heat tortillas according to package directions. Spread each tortilla with ¼ cup refried beans and sprinkle with lettuce. Place 1 burger in center of each tortilla and sprinkle with 1 tablespoon cheese. Fold sides of tortillas over burgers to create burritos. Serve with salsa, if desired.   *Makes 8 servings*

*Favorite recipe from **National Turkey Federation***

Turkey Enchilada Pie

¾ **pound ground turkey**
2 **teaspoons vegetable oil**
1 **can (14½ ounces) DEL MONTE® Zesty Diced Tomatoes with Mild Green Chilies**
1 **package (1¼ ounces) taco seasoning mix**
½ **cup sliced green onions**
1 **can (2¼ ounces) sliced ripe olives, drained**
6 **corn tortillas**
1½ **cups shredded sharp Cheddar cheese**

1. Brown meat in oil in large skillet over medium-high heat. Stir in tomatoes and taco seasoning mix.

2. Reduce heat; cover and cook 10 minutes, stirring occasionally. Stir in green onions and olives.

3. Place 1 tortilla in bottom of 2-quart baking dish; cover with about ½ cup meat sauce. Top with about ¼ cup cheese. Repeat, making a six-layer stack.

4. Pour ½ cup water down edge, into bottom of dish. Cover with foil and bake at 425°F, 30 minutes or until heated through. Cut into 4 wedges. Garnish with sour cream, if desired.   *Makes 4 servings*

Prep Time: 15 minutes
Cook Time: 48 minutes

Turkey Enchilada Pie

Turkey & Zucchini Enchiladas with Tomatillo-Green Chile Sauce

1¼ pound turkey leg
1 tablespoon olive oil
1 small onion, thinly sliced
1 tablespoon minced garlic
1 pound zucchini, quartered lengthwise and sliced thinly crosswise
1½ teaspoons cumin
½ teaspoon dried oregano leaves
¾ cup (3 ounces) shredded reduced-fat Monterey Jack cheese
12 (6-inch) corn tortillas
Tomatillo-Green Chile Sauce (recipe page 110)
½ cup crumbled feta cheese
6 sprigs fresh cilantro for garnish

1. Place turkey in large saucepan; cover with water. Bring to a boil over high heat. Reduce heat to medium-low. Cover and simmer 1½ to 2 hours or until meat pulls apart easily when tested with fork. Drain; discard skin and bone. Cut meat into small pieces. Place in medium bowl; set aside.

2. Preheat oven to 350°F.

3. Heat oil over medium-high heat in large skillet. Add onion; cook and stir 3 to 4 minutes or until tender. Reduce heat to medium. Add garlic; cook and stir 3 to 4 minutes or until onion is golden. Add zucchini, 2 tablespoons water, cumin and oregano. Cover; cook and stir over medium heat 10 minutes or until zucchini is tender. Add to turkey. Stir in Monterey Jack cheese.

4. Heat large nonstick skillet over medium-high heat. Place 1 inch water in medium bowl. Dip 1 tortilla in water; shake off excess. Place in hot skillet. Cook 10 to 15 seconds on each side or until tortilla is hot and pliable. Repeat with remaining tortillas.

5. Spray bottom of 13×9-inch baking pan with nonstick cooking spray. Spoon ¼ cup filling in center of each tortilla; fold sides over to enclose. Place seam side down in pan. Brush tops with ½ cup Tomatillo-Green Chile Sauce. Cover; bake 30 to 40 minutes or until heated through. Top enchiladas with remaining Tomatillo-Green Chile Sauce and feta cheese. Garnish with cilantro.

Makes 6 servings

continued on page 110

Turkey & Zucchini Enchiladas with Tomatillo-Green Chile Sauce

Tomatillo-Green Chile Sauce

¾ **pound fresh tomatillos** *or* **2 cans (18 ounces each) whole tomatillos, drained**
½ **cup reduced-sodium chicken broth**
1 can (4 ounces) diced mild green chilies, drained
½ **teaspoon ground cumin**
1 teaspoon dried oregano leaves, crushed
2 tablespoons chopped fresh cilantro (optional)

1. If using fresh tomatillos, remove husks; wash thoroughly. Place tomatillos in large saucepan; cover with water. Bring to a boil over high heat. Reduce heat to medium-high and simmer gently 20 to 30 minutes or until tomatillos are tender.

2. Place tomatillos, chilies, broth (omit if using canned tomatillos), cumin and oregano in food processor or blender; process until smooth. Return mixture to pan. Cover; heat over medium heat until bubbling. Stir in cilantro, if desired. *Makes about 3 cups*

Chili Roasted Turkey Breast

1 envelope LIPTON® RECIPE SECRETS® Onion Soup Mix*
¼ **cup BERTOLLI® Olive Oil**
1½ **teaspoons chili powder**
1½ **teaspoons fresh lime juice**
½ **teaspoon garlic powder (optional)**
½ **teaspoon ground cumin**
¼ **teaspoon dried oregano leaves**
1 (5-pound) turkey breast (with bone)

*Also terrific with LIPTON® RECIPE SECRETS® Onion Mushroom or Beefy Onion Soup Mix.

Preheat oven to 350°F. In small bowl, blend all ingredients except turkey; let stand 5 minutes. In large roasting pan, place turkey, breast side up. Brush soup mixture onto turkey; tent with aluminum foil. Roast 1 hour, basting once. Remove foil and continue roasting 1 hour or until meat thermometer reaches 180°F. Let stand, tented with foil, 10 minutes. *Makes about 6 servings*

Mexican Turkey Rice

½ cup chopped onion
⅓ cup long-grain rice
1 clove garlic, minced
1 tablespoon olive oil
1 can (16 ounces) reduced-sodium stewed tomatoes, coarsely chopped
½ cup reduced-sodium chicken bouillon
1 teaspoon chili powder
½ teaspoon dried oregano leaves
⅛ teaspoon crushed red pepper
⅓ cup chopped green bell pepper
1 pound fully-cooked oven-roasted turkey breast, cut into ¼-inch cubes

1. In large nonstick skillet over medium-high heat, cook and stir onion, rice and garlic in oil 3 to 4 minutes or until rice is lightly browned. Stir in tomatoes, bouillon, chili powder, oregano and crushed red pepper. Bring to a boil. Reduce heat to low; cover and simmer 15 minutes.

2. Stir in bell pepper and turkey. Cover; cook 3 to 4 minutes or until mixture is heated through.

Makes 6 servings

Favorite recipe from **National Turkey Federation**

Turkey and Bean Tostadas

6 (8-inch) flour tortillas
1 pound 93% fat-free ground turkey
1 can (15 ounces) chili beans in chili sauce
½ teaspoon chili powder
3 cups washed and shredded romaine lettuce
1 large tomato, chopped
¼ cup chopped fresh cilantro
¼ cup (1 ounce) shredded reduced-fat Monterey Jack cheese
½ cup low-fat sour cream (optional)

1. Preheat oven to 350°F. Place tortillas on baking sheets. Bake 7 minutes or until crisp. Place on individual plates.

2. Heat large nonstick skillet over medium-high heat until hot. Add turkey. Cook and stir until turkey is browned; drain. Add beans and chili powder. Cook 5 minutes over medium heat. Divide turkey mixture evenly among tortillas. Top with remaining ingredients. *Makes 6 servings*

Prep and Cook Time: 20 minutes

Turkey and Bean Tostadas

Turkey-Tortilla Bake

9 (6-inch) corn tortillas
½ pound 93% fat-free ground turkey
½ cup chopped onion
¾ cup mild or medium taco sauce
1 can (4 ounces) chopped green chilies, drained
½ cup frozen corn, thawed
½ cup (2 ounces) shredded reduced-fat Cheddar cheese

1. Preheat oven to 400°F. Place tortillas on large baking sheet, overlapping tortillas as little as possible. Bake 4 minutes; turn tortillas. Continue baking 2 minutes or until crisp. Cool completely on wire rack.

2. Heat medium nonstick skillet over medium heat until hot. Add turkey and onion. Cook and stir 5 minutes or until turkey is browned and onion is tender. Add taco sauce, chilies and corn. Reduce heat and simmer 5 minutes.

3. Break 3 tortillas and arrange over bottom of 1½-quart casserole. Spoon half the turkey mixture over tortillas; sprinkle with half the cheese. Repeat layers. Bake 10 minutes or until cheese is melted and casserole is heated through. Break remaining tortillas and sprinkle over casserole. Garnish with sour cream, if desired.   *Makes 4 servings*

Prep and Cook Time: 30 minutes

Turkey-Tortilla Bake

Turkey Mole

2½ pounds turkey legs
¼ cup sliced or slivered almonds, or unsalted roasted peanuts
2 tablespoons sesame seeds
   Mole Sauce (recipe page 117)
¼ to ½ teaspoon sugar (optional)
¼ cup chopped fresh cilantro
3 cups cooked rice

1. Place turkey legs in stockpot or Dutch oven; cover with water. Bring to a boil over high heat. Reduce heat to medium. Cover; simmer 1½ hours or until meat is tender; drain. Cool slightly. Remove skin, bones and fat; discard. Cut turkey into large cubes.

2. Heat large nonstick skillet over medium heat. Add almonds. Cook, stirring often, 4 to 5 minutes or until golden. Transfer almonds to small bowl. Add sesame seeds to skillet. Cook and stir 4 to 5 minutes or until golden. Set 2 teaspoons aside for garnish; add remaining sesame seeds to almonds. Reserve for Mole Sauce.

3. Prepare Mole Sauce.

4. Combine turkey and Mole Sauce in large nonstick skillet. Bring to a simmer over medium-high heat. Cover and simmer 10 minutes or until turkey is hot. Add water or additional broth if too thick; simmer uncovered if thin. Add sugar, if desired. Sprinkle with reserved sesame seeds and cilantro. Serve over rice. Garnish as desired. *Makes 8 servings*

Mole Sauce

1 tablespoon olive oil
1 small onion, chopped
¼ cup chili powder
4 cloves garlic, minced
1 teaspoon ground cinnamon
½ teaspoon ground cloves
½ teaspoon anise seeds or fennel seeds
1 large tomato, seeded and chopped
⅓ cup raisins
 Reserved almond mixture from Turkey Mole (recipe page 116)
1 large ripe banana, cut into 1-inch pieces
1 corn or flour tortilla, torn into pieces, or 1 slice bread, torn into pieces
2 cups reduced-sodium chicken broth, divided
1 square (1 ounce) semisweet chocolate

1. Heat oil over medium heat in large nonstick skillet. Add onion. Cook and stir 5 minutes or until tender. Add chili powder, garlic, cinnamon, cloves and anise seeds. Cook and stir 3 minutes or until mixture is dry and somewhat darker. Add tomato and raisins. Cover; cook 3 minutes or until tomato is tender.

2. Pour mixture into food processor with reserved almond mixture. Add banana, tortilla and ½ cup broth; process until puréed. Return to skillet over medium heat and bring to a simmer. Add chocolate; stir until melted. Add remaining 1½ cups broth; reduce heat to low. Cover; simmer 20 minutes, stirring occasionally, to allow flavors to blend. *Makes about 3 cups*

Poached Turkey with Ancho Chili Sauce

2 turkey tenderloins (½ pound each) *or* **1 pound boneless turkey breast**
1 ancho chili pepper, seeded and stemmed
1¼ cups water
3 cloves garlic, peeled
1 cup roasted red peppers, coarsely chopped
1 teaspoon salt
½ teaspoon dried oregano leaves, crushed
3 cups hot cooked rice
4 green onions, finely chopped

1. Place turkey tenderloins in Dutch oven or stockpot; add enough water to cover. Bring to a boil over high heat.

2. Reduce heat to medium; cover and simmer 20 minutes or until turkey is no longer pink in center. Remove from Dutch oven; cover to keep warm. Let stand 15 minutes before slicing.

3. Meanwhile, combine ancho chili, 1¼ cups water and garlic in small saucepan; bring to a boil over high heat. Cover and turn off heat; let stand 15 minutes.

4. Add roasted red peppers, salt and oregano to chili mixture. Transfer mixture to food processor or blender; process until sauce is smooth.

5. Combine rice and green onions, reserving 2 tablespoons green onion for garnish. Arrange turkey over rice. Top with chili sauce and sprinkle with reserved green onion before serving. Garnish as desired.   *Makes 4 servings*

Poached Turkey
with Ancho Chili Sauce

Turkey Fajitas

½ cup sliced green onions
½ cup lemon juice
½ cup honey
½ cup warm water
3 tablespoons vegetable oil
1 clove garlic, minced
1 (1-pound) package turkey breast slices, cut into $2 \times \frac{3}{4}$-inch strips
1 medium yellow or green bell pepper, cut into strips
1 medium tomato, chopped
½ cup chopped fresh cilantro
4 (8-inch) flour tortillas
  Picante sauce

Combine green onions, lemon juice, honey and water in small bowl; set aside. Heat oil and garlic in large skillet over medium-high heat. Add turkey; cook and stir for 2 minutes. Add pepper strips and lemon juice mixture; continue to cook and stir until liquid evaporates and turkey is golden brown. Stir in tomato and cilantro. Spoon mixture onto tortillas. Fold in half or roll up. Serve with picante sauce.

Makes 4 servings

Turkey Fajitas

Beef

Steak Ranchero

⅔ cup A.1.® Steak Sauce
⅔ cup mild, medium or hot thick and chunky salsa
2 tablespoons lime juice
1 (1-pound) beef top round steak, about ¾ inch thick
⅓ cup sliced ripe olives
4 cups shredded lettuce
⅓ cup dairy sour cream

Blend steak sauce, salsa and lime juice. Place steak in glass dish; coat both sides with ½ cup salsa mixture. Cover; refrigerate 1 hour, turning occasionally.

Heat remaining salsa mixture in small saucepan over medium heat. Reserve 2 tablespoons olives for garnish; stir remaining olives into sauce. Keep warm.

Remove steak from marinade; discard marinade. Grill over medium heat for 6 minutes on each side or until done, turning once.

To serve, arrange lettuce on serving platter. Thinly slice steak across grain; arrange over lettuce. Top with warm sauce and sour cream. Garnish with reserved olive slices.   *Makes 4 servings*

Steak Ranchero

Double Duty Tacos

Mexicali Chili Rub
- ¼ cup chili powder
- 3 tablespoons garlic salt
- 2 tablespoons ground cumin
- 2 tablespoons dried oregano leaves
- ½ teaspoon ground red pepper

Tacos
- 2 pounds lean ground beef
- 1 large onion, chopped
- 3 tablespoons Mexicali Chili Rub
- ¾ cup water
- 2 tablespoons tomato paste
- 16 packaged crispy taco shells
- 2 cups (8 ounces) shredded Monterey Jack or taco seasoned cojack cheese
- 2 cups shredded lettuce
- 1 cup chopped tomatoes
- 1 cup diced ripe avocado
- ½ cup light or regular sour cream
- Prepared salsa

1. For rub, combine chili powder, garlic salt, cumin, oregano and ground red pepper in small bowl; mix well. Transfer to container with tight-fitting lid. Store in cool dry place up to 2 months.

2. Cook beef and onion in large deep skillet over medium-high heat until no longer pink. Pour off drippings. Sprinkle chili rub over beef mixture; cook 1 minute. Reduce heat to medium. Add water and tomato paste. Cover; simmer 5 minutes.

3. Spoon beef mixture into taco shells; top with cheese. Arrange lettuce, tomatoes, avocado, sour cream and salsa in bowls. Serve tacos with toppings as desired.   *Makes 8 servings*

Serving Suggestion: Serve with refried beans or Spanish rice.

Prep and Cook Time: 20 minutes

Double Duty Tacos

Layered Mexican Casserole

8 ounces ground beef
1 (12-ounce) can whole kernel corn, drained
1 (12-ounce) jar chunky salsa
1 (2¼-ounce) can sliced pitted ripe olives, drained
1 cup cream-style cottage cheese
1 (8-ounce) carton dairy sour cream
5 cups tortilla chips (7 to 8 ounces)
2 cups (8 ounces) shredded Wisconsin Cheddar cheese, divided
½ cup chopped tomato

Brown ground beef in large skillet; drain. Add corn and salsa; cook until thoroughly heated. Reserve 2 tablespoons olives; stir remaining olives into beef mixture. Combine cottage cheese and sour cream in bowl.

In 2-quart casserole, layer 2 cups chips, half of meat mixture, ¾ cup Cheddar cheese and half of cottage cheese mixture. Repeat layers; cover. Bake in preheated 350°F oven, 35 minutes. Line edge of casserole with remaining 1 cup chips; top with tomato, reserved 2 tablespoons olives and remaining ½ cup Cheddar cheese. Bake 10 minutes or until cheese is melted and chips are hot.

Makes 4 to 6 servings

Favorite recipe from **Wisconsin Milk Marketing Board**

Layered Mexican Casserole

Beef Fajitas

1¾ cups (16-ounce jar) ORTEGA® Salsa Prima-Thick & Chunky Mild
¼ cup vegetable oil, *divided*
2 tablespoons chopped fresh cilantro
1 tablespoon chili powder
2 large cloves garlic, finely chopped
½ teaspoon ground cumin
½ teaspoon salt
1 pound sirloin steak, cut into 2-inch strips
1 cup (1 small) red bell pepper strips
1 cup (1 small) green bell pepper strips
1 cup (1 small) sliced onion
   Flour tortillas, warmed
   Sour cream

COMBINE salsa, *2 tablespoons* oil, cilantro, chili powder, garlic, cumin and salt in large bowl. Add beef; cover. Marinate in refrigerator for at least 1 hour.

HEAT *remaining* vegetable oil in large skillet over medium-high heat. Add bell peppers and onion; cook for 5 to 6 minutes or until onions are slightly golden and peppers are tender. Add beef mixture; cook, stirring occasionally, for 7 to 8 minutes or until meat is no longer pink.

SERVE in tortillas; top with sour cream.   *Makes 6 to 8 servings*

Cowpoke Enchiladas

1⅓ cups tomato salsa
1 cup HEINZ® Tomato Ketchup
½ pound lean ground beef
½ cup chopped onion
½ cup chopped green bell pepper
1 can (15½ ounces) pinto or kidney beans, drained
6 (8-inch) flour tortillas, warmed
1¼ cups shredded Cheddar cheese, divided

In small bowl, combine salsa and ketchup. Pour ½ cup salsa mixture into bottom of 13×9-inch baking pan; set remainder aside. In large nonstick skillet, brown beef with onion and bell pepper; drain fat. Add beans and ⅓ cup salsa mixture; mix well. Spoon ½ cup beef mixture onto each tortilla; sprinkle with 2 tablespoons cheese. Roll tortillas; place seam-side down in prepared baking pan. Spoon remaining salsa mixture over tortillas; sprinkle with remaining ½ cup cheese. Cover; bake in 350°F oven, 35 to 40 minutes or until hot.

Makes 6 servings

Wild Rice & Beef Quesadillas

1⅓ cups shredded Monterey Jack cheese
1 cup cooked wild rice
½ cup minced fresh cilantro
2 teaspoons Dijon mustard
8 (6-inch) flour tortillas
1 cup thinly sliced sweet onion
1 cup thinly sliced green bell pepper
8 thin slices deli roast beef
Prepared salsa
Fresh Cilantro Leaves

In medium bowl, combine cheese, wild rice, cilantro and mustard; spread on 4 tortillas. Layer each with onion, bell pepper and beef; top with another tortilla. Preheat skillet over medium heat; spray with nonstick cooking spray. Fry quesadillas 2 to 3 minutes. Spray top of tortillas with cooking spray; turn gently and cook until cheese melts. Cut into wedges and top with salsa and cilantro.

Makes 4 main servings or 16 appetizers

Favorite recipe from **Minnesota Cultivated Wild Rice Council**

Speedy Beef & Bean Burritos

8 flour tortillas (7-inch)
1 pound ground beef
1 cup chopped onion
1 teaspoon bottled minced garlic
1 can (15 ounces) black beans, drained and rinsed
1 cup spicy thick and chunky salsa
2 teaspoons ground cumin
1 bunch cilantro
2 cups (8 ounces) shredded cojack or Monterey Jack cheese

1. Wrap tortillas in foil; place on center rack in oven. Heat oven to 350°F; heat tortillas 15 minutes.

2. While tortillas are warming, prepare burrito filling. Combine beef, onion and garlic in large skillet; cook over medium-high heat until beef is no longer pink, breaking beef apart with wooden spoon. Pour off drippings.

3. Stir beans, salsa and cumin into beef mixture; reduce heat to medium. Cover and simmer 10 minutes, stirring once.

4. While filling is simmering, chop enough cilantro to measure ¼ cup. Stir into filling. Spoon filling down centers of warm tortillas; top with cheese. Roll up and serve immediately.   *Makes 4 servings*

Prep and Cook Time: 20 minutes

Speedy Beef & Bean Burritos

Mexican Beef Stir-Fry

1 pound beef flank steak
2 tablespoons vegetable oil
1 teaspoon ground cumin
1 teaspoon dried oregano leaves
1 clove garlic, crushed
1 red or green bell pepper, cut into thin strips
1 medium onion, cut into thin wedges
1 to 2 jalapeño peppers,* thinly sliced
3 cups thinly sliced lettuce

*Remove interior ribs and seeds if a milder flavor is desired. Jalapeño peppers can sting and irritate the skin; wear rubber gloves when handling peppers and do not touch eyes. Wash hands after handling peppers.

Cut beef steak into $1/8$-inch-thick strips. Combine oil, cumin, oregano and garlic in small bowl. Heat $1/2$ oil mixture in large nonstick skillet over medium-high heat. Add bell pepper, onion and jalapeño pepper; stir-fry 2 to 3 minutes or until crisp-tender. Remove and reserve. In same skillet, stir-fry beef strips ($1/2$ at a time) in remaining oil mixture 1 to 2 minutes. Return vegetables to skillet and heat through. Serve beef mixture over lettuce. *Makes 4 servings*

Tip: Recipe may also be prepared using beef top sirloin or top round steak cut 1 inch thick.

Serving Suggestion: Serve with corn bread twists.

Favorite recipe from **North Dakota Beef Commission**

Mexican Beef Stir-Fry

Fajitas

½ cup chopped onion
¼ cup GRANDMA'S® Molasses
¼ cup oil
2 tablespoons ROSE'S® Lime Juice
2 tablespoons chili powder
½ teaspoon oregano leaves
2 garlic cloves, minced
1 pound boneless top round or sirloin steak, cut into thin strips
10 flour tortillas (8 to 10 inches), softened
½ cup (4 ounces) shredded Monterey Jack cheese
2 cups refried beans
2 tomatoes, chopped
1½ cups shredded lettuce
1 avocado, chopped
1 cup salsa
Sour cream

1. In medium plastic bowl, combine onion, molasses, oil, lime juice, chili powder, oregano and garlic. Mix well. Add steak, stir to coat. Cover; marinate 4 to 6 hours or overnight, stirring occasionally.

2. In large skillet, stir-fry meat mixture 5 minutes or until brown. To serve, place meat in center of each tortilla; top with cheese, refried beans, tomatoes, lettuce, avocado and salsa. Fold up tortilla. Serve with sour cream.

Makes 5 servings

Fajitas

Tijuana Tacos

1 teaspoon vegetable oil
½ cup chopped green bell pepper
½ cup chopped green onions
1 jalapeño pepper,* minced
1 pound lean ground beef
1 cup salsa
½ teaspoon ground cumin
½ teaspoon chili powder
8 taco shells
2 cups shredded lettuce
2 cups chopped tomato
1½ cups (6 ounces) shredded Cheddar cheese

*Jalapeño peppers can sting and irritate the skin; wear rubber gloves when handling peppers and do not touch eyes. Wash hands after handling peppers.

Heat oil in large nonstick skillet over medium-high heat until hot. Add bell pepper, onions and jalapeño pepper; cook and stir 5 minutes or until vegetables are tender.

Add beef to vegetable mixture. Cook until no longer pink; pour off excess fat. Add salsa, cumin and chili powder to meat mixture; stir to combine.

Spoon beef mixture into taco shells. Top with lettuce, tomato and Cheddar cheese. Garnish as desired.

Makes 8 servings

Tijuana Tacos

Mexican Steak with Chimichurri Sauce

⅔ cup olive oil
½ cup minced fresh parsley
⅓ cup *Frank's® RedHot®* Cayenne Pepper Sauce
3 tablespoons lime juice
1 tablespoon *French's®* Worcestershire Sauce
2 teaspoons dried oregano leaves
2 cloves garlic, minced
2 pounds boneless beef sirloin (1½ inches thick)

Place oil, parsley, **Frank's RedHot** Sauce, lime juice, Worcestershire, oregano and garlic in blender or food processor. Cover and process until well blended. Reserve ⅔ cup sauce mixture. Place steak in large resealable plastic food storage bag. Pour remaining sauce mixture over steak. Seal bag and marinate in refrigerator 30 minutes.

Place steak on grid, discarding marinade. Grill over hot coals 10 minutes per side for medium-rare or to desired doneness. Let steak stand 5 minutes. Slice steak diagonally. Serve with reserved sauce mixture.

Makes 6 to 8 servings

Prep Time: 10 minutes
Marinate Time: 30 minutes
Cook Time: 20 minutes

Beef Mole Tamale Pie

1½ pounds ground chuck
1 medium onion, chopped
1 green bell pepper, chopped
2 cloves garlic, minced
1¼ cups medium-hot salsa
1 package (10 ounces) frozen whole kernel corn, partially thawed
1 tablespoon unsweetened cocoa powder
2 teaspoons ground cumin
1 teaspoon dried oregano leaves
1½ teaspoons salt, divided
¼ teaspoon ground cinnamon
2 cups (8 ounces) shredded Monterey Jack or Cheddar cheese
⅓ cup chopped fresh cilantro
1 cup all-purpose flour
¾ cup yellow cornmeal
3 tablespoons sugar
2 teaspoons baking powder
⅔ cup milk
3 tablespoons butter, melted
1 egg, beaten
Cilantro leaves, chili pepper and sour cream for garnish

Preheat oven to 400°F. Spray 11×7-inch baking dish with nonstick cooking spray. Brown ground chuck with onion, bell pepper and garlic in large deep skillet or Dutch oven over medium heat until meat just loses its pink color. Pour off drippings. Stir in salsa, corn, cocoa, cumin, oregano, 1 teaspoon salt and cinnamon. Bring to a boil. Reduce heat to medium-low; simmer, uncovered, 8 minutes, stirring occasionally. Remove from heat; stir in cheese and cilantro. Spread in prepared dish.

Combine flour, cornmeal, sugar, baking powder and remaining ½ teaspoon salt in large bowl. Add milk, butter and egg; stir just until dry ingredients are moistened. Drop by spoonfuls evenly over meat mixture; spread batter evenly with spatula.

Bake 15 minutes. *Reduce oven temperature to 350°F.* Bake 20 minutes or until topping is light brown and filling is bubbly. Let stand 5 minutes before serving. Garnish, if desired.   *Makes 6 servings*

30-Minute Chili Olé

1 cup chopped onion
2 cloves garlic, minced
1 tablespoon vegetable oil
2 pounds ground beef
1 (15-ounce) can tomato sauce
1 (14½-ounce) can stewed tomatoes
¾ cup A.1.® Steak Sauce
1 tablespoon chili powder
1 teaspoon ground cumin
1 (16-ounce) can black beans, rinsed and drained
1 (11-ounce) can corn, drained
Shredded cheese, sour cream and chopped tomato, for garnish

Sauté onion and garlic in oil in 6-quart heavy pot over medium-high heat until tender.

Add beef; cook and stir until brown. Drain; stir in tomato sauce, stewed tomatoes, steak sauce, chili powder and cumin.

Heat to a boil; reduce heat to low. Cover; simmer for 10 minutes, stirring occasionally. Stir in beans and corn; simmer, uncovered, for 10 minutes.

Serve hot, garnished with cheese, sour cream and tomatoes.   *Makes 8 servings*

Southwest Steak

¾ **cup Italian dressing**
½ **cup minced fresh parsley**
⅓ **cup Frank's® RedHot® Cayenne Pepper Sauce**
3 **tablespoons lime juice**
1 **tablespoon French's® Worcestershire Sauce**
2 **pounds boneless sirloin or top round steak (1½ inches thick)**

1. Place dressing, parsley, **Frank's RedHot** Sauce, lime juice and Worcestershire in blender or food processor. Cover; process until smooth. Reserve ⅔ cup sauce. Pour remaining sauce over steak in deep dish. Cover; refrigerate 30 minutes.

2. Grill or broil steak 8 minutes per side for medium-rare or to desired doneness. Let stand 5 minutes. Slice steak and serve with reserved sauce. *Makes 6 to 8 servings*

Prep Time: 10 minutes
Marinate Time: 30 minutes
Cook Time: 20 minutes

Southwest Steak

Tasty Taco Burgers

1 pound ground beef
1 package (1¼ ounces) taco seasoning mix
8 KRAFT® American Singles Pasteurized Process Cheese Food
4 Kaiser rolls, split
  Lettuce leaves
  Salsa
  BREAKSTONE'S® or KNUDSEN® Sour Cream (optional)

MIX 1 pound ground beef and taco seasoning mix. Shape into 4 patties.

GRILL patties over hot coals 6 to 8 minutes on each side or to desired doneness. Top each patty with 2 process cheese food slices. Continue grilling until process cheese food is melted.

FILL rolls with lettuce and cheeseburgers. Top with salsa and sour cream, if desired.

Makes 4 servings

Señor Says: **Tasty Taco Burgers are wonderful treats. For a Mexican flare, serve with tortilla chips instead of the traditional side dish, French fries.**

Tasty Taco Burger

Beef Picante and Sour Cream Casserole

6 ounces uncooked wagon wheel pasta

8 ounces 95% lean ground beef

1½ cups reduced-sodium mild picante sauce

1 cup red kidney beans, rinsed and drained

¾ cup water

1 tablespoon chili powder

1 teaspoon ground cumin

½ cup nonfat cottage cheese

½ cup nonfat sour cream

½ cup chopped green onions, with tops

1 can (2¼ ounces) sliced black olives

¼ cup chopped fresh cilantro or fresh parsley

1. Preheat oven to 325°F. Spray 9-inch square baking pan with nonstick cooking spray; set aside. Cook pasta according to package directions, omitting salt. Drain. Place in bottom of prepared pan; set aside.

2. Brown beef in large nonstick skillet over medium-high heat 4 to 5 minutes or until no longer pink, stirring to separate beef; drain fat.

3. Add picante sauce, beans, water, chili powder and cumin; blend well. Bring to a boil over high heat. Reduce heat to low; simmer, covered, 20 minutes.

4. Combine cottage cheese, sour cream and green onions in food processor or blender; process until smooth. Spread cottage cheese mixture over pasta in prepared pan. Spoon meat mixture over cottage cheese mixture; cover with foil. Bake 20 minutes or until heated through. Remove from oven; let stand 10 minutes to allow flavors to blend. Top with olives and cilantro.   *Makes 4 servings*

Special Beef and Spinach Burritos

1 pound lean ground beef
1 small onion, chopped
1 clove garlic, crushed
½ teaspoon salt
½ teaspoon chili powder
¼ teaspoon ground cumin
¼ teaspoon black pepper
1 package (10 ounces) frozen chopped spinach, thawed, well drained
2 jalapeño peppers,* seeded, finely chopped
1½ cups (6 ounces) shredded Monterey Jack cheese
4 large (10-inch) *or* 8 medium (8-inch) flour tortillas, warmed
  Lime slices (optional)
  Jalapeño pepper slices (optional)
1 cup prepared chunky salsa

*Jalapeño peppers can sting and irritate the skin; wear rubber gloves when handling peppers and do not touch eyes. Wash hands after handling peppers.

In large nonstick skillet, brown beef, onion and garlic over medium heat 8 to 10 minutes or until beef is no longer pink, stirring occasionally. Pour off drippings. Season with salt, chili powder, cumin and black pepper. Stir in spinach and jalapeño peppers; heat through. Remove from heat; stir in cheese.

To serve, spoon equal amount of beef mixture into center of each tortilla. Fold bottom edge up over filling. Fold right and left sides to center, overlapping edges. Garnish with lime and jalapeño slices, if desired. Serve with salsa.

Makes 4 servings

Favorite recipe from **North Dakota Beef Commission**

Fiesta Beef Enchiladas

8 ounces 93% lean ground beef
½ cup sliced green onions
2 teaspoons fresh minced or bottled garlic
1 cup cold cooked white or brown rice
1½ cups chopped tomato, divided
¾ cup frozen corn, thawed
1 cup (4 ounces) shredded reduced-fat Mexican cheese blend or Cheddar cheese, divided
½ cup salsa or picante sauce
12 (6- to 7-inch) corn tortillas
1 can (10 ounces) mild or hot enchilada sauce
1 cup sliced romaine lettuce leaves

1. Preheat oven to 375°F. Spray 13×9-inch baking dish with nonstick cooking spray. Set aside. Cook ground beef in medium nonstick skillet over medium heat until no longer pink; drain. Add green onions and garlic; cook and stir 2 minutes.

2. Combine meat mixture, rice, 1 cup tomato, corn, ½ cup cheese and salsa; mix well. Spoon mixture down center of tortillas. Roll up; place seam side down in prepared pan. Spoon enchilada sauce evenly over enchiladas.

3. Cover with foil; bake for 20 minutes or until hot. Sprinkle with remaining ½ cup cheese; bake 5 minutes or until cheese melts. Top with lettuce and remaining ½ cup tomato.   *Makes 4 servings*

Prep Time: 15 minutes
Cook Time: 35 minutes

Fiesta Beef Enchiladas

Original Ortega® Taco Recipe

1 pound ground beef
1 package (1¼ ounces) ORTEGA® Taco Seasoning Mix
¾ cup water
1 package (12) ORTEGA® Taco Shells, warmed
Toppings: shredded lettuce, chopped tomatoes, shredded mild Cheddar cheese, ORTEGA® Thick & Smooth Taco Sauce

BROWN beef; drain. Stir in seasoning mix and water. Bring to a boil. Reduce heat to low; cook, stirring occasionally, for 5 to 6 minutes or until mixture is thickened.

FILL taco shells with beef mixture. Top with lettuce, tomatoes, cheese and taco sauce.

Makes 6 servings

Señor Says: **To easily warm taco shells, place in preheated 350°F oven for 5 minutes.**

Gazpacho Steak Roll

        1 (2-pound) beef flank steak, butterflied
    ⅔ cup A.1.® Steak Sauce, divided
        1 cup (4 ounces) shredded Monterey Jack cheese
    ½ cup chopped tomato
    ⅓ cup chopped cucumber
    ¼ cup chopped green bell pepper
        2 tablespoons sliced green onion

Open butterflied steak like a book on smooth surface and flatten slightly. Spread ⅓ cup steak sauce over surface. Layer remaining ingredients over sauce. Roll up steak from short edge; secure with wooden toothpicks or tie with string if necessary.

Grill steak roll over medium heat 30 to 40 minutes or to desired doneness, turning and brushing often with remaining steak sauce during last 10 minutes of cooking. Remove toothpicks; slice and serve garnished as desired. *Makes 8 servings*

Chili-Stuffed Poblano Peppers

        1 pound lean ground beef
        4 large poblano peppers halved lengthwise, seeded and stemmed
        1 can (15 ounces) chili-seasoned beans
        1 can (14½ ounces) chili-style chunky tomatoes, undrained
        1 tablespoon Mexican (adobo) seasoning
    ⅔ cup shredded Mexican cheese blend or Monterey Jack cheese

1. Bring 2 quarts water to a boil in 3-quart saucepan. Cook ground beef in large nonstick skillet over medium-high heat 5 to 6 minutes or until no longer pink. While meat is cooking, place pepper halves in boiling water; cook 3 minutes or until bright green and slightly softened. Remove; drain upside down on plate.

2. Preheat broiler. Add beans, tomatoes and Mexican seasoning to ground beef. Cook and stir over medium heat 5 minutes or until mixture thickens slightly. Arrange peppers, cut side up, in 13×9-inch baking dish. Divide chili mixture evenly among each pepper; top with cheese. Broil 6 inches from heat 1 minute or until cheese is melted. Serve immediately. *Makes 4 servings*

Gazpacho Steak Roll

Chimichangas

Spiced Meat Filling (recipe page 155)
1 cup refried beans
1 cup (4 ounces) shredded Monterey Jack cheese
8 (10- or 12-inch) flour tortillas
Vegetable oil for deep-frying

Condiments
1 small head lettuce, shredded
2 tomatoes, diced
1 cup (½ pint) sour cream
1 cup salsa or picante sauce
1 can (2¼ ounces) sliced pitted black olives, drained
8 radishes, sliced

Prepare Spiced Meat Filling. To assemble each chimichanga, spoon about 2 tablespoons beans, 2 tablespoons cheese and ¼ cup meat filling into center of each tortilla. Fold 1 side of tortilla over filling; fold in ends, then roll to enclose ends and filling. Secure open edge with wooden toothpick. Pour oil into large, deep skillet to depth of 1 inch. Place over medium heat until oil registers 350°F on deep-frying thermometer. Lower 1 chimichanga into oil, seam side down. Add second chimichanga. Cook 1 minute or until golden brown. Carefully turn over; continue cooking 1 minute or until golden. Remove from oil; drain on paper towels. Keep warm in 200°F oven; repeat until all chimichangas are cooked. To serve, place 1 chimichanga on dinner plate; remove wooden toothpick. Serve with condiments as desired.

Makes 8 chimichangas

Señor Says: **If a deep-fat thermometer is not available, drop a cube of white bread in the hot oil. The bread will brown evenly in 1 minute at approximately 350° to 360°F, 40 seconds at 365° to 375°F, and 20 seconds at 380° to 390°F.**

Spiced Meat Filling

½ pound lean ground beef
¼ pound lean ground pork
½ cup chopped onion
1 clove garlic, minced
1 jalapeño pepper,* stemmed, seeded and minced
1 teaspoon brown sugar
1 teaspoon chili powder
¼ teaspoon salt
¼ teaspoon dried oregano
¼ teaspoon ground cumin
⅛ teaspoon ground cinnamon
½ cup canned tomatoes, drained and finely chopped
1 tablespoon cider vinegar

*Jalapeño peppers can sting and irritate the skin; wear rubber gloves when handling peppers and do not touch eyes. Wash hands after handling peppers.

Crumble beef and pork into large skillet; stir over medium-high heat until browned. Add onion, garlic and jalapeño pepper. Reduce heat to medium; cook until onion is tender. Spoon off and discard pan drippings. Add remaining ingredients. Simmer, stirring occasionally, 15 minutes or until most of liquid has evaporated.

Velveeta® Beef Enchiladas Olé

1 pound ground beef or 1 pound boneless skinless chicken breasts, chopped

1 cup TACO BELL® HOME ORIGINALS®* Thick 'N Chunky Salsa, divided

1 pound (16 ounces) VELVEETA® Mexican Pasteurized Process Cheese Spread with Jalapeño Peppers, cut up, divided

10 flour tortillas

*TACO BELL and HOME ORIGINALS are registered trademarks owned and licensed by Taco Bell Corp.

1. Brown meat; drain. Stir in ½ cup of the salsa and ½ of the Velveeta; cook and stir on medium-low heat until Velveeta is melted.

2. Spoon ¼ cup meat mixture in center of each tortilla; roll up. Place tortillas, seam-side down, in microwavable baking dish. Top with remaining ½ cup salsa and Velveeta. Cover loosely with microwavable plastic wrap.

3. Microwave on HIGH 4 to 6 minutes or until Velveeta is melted.   *Makes 5 servings*

Prep Time: 20 minutes
Microwave Time: 6 minutes

 Señor Says: **Flour tortillas come in many colors and sizes. You'll find them in the refrigerated dairy case or grocery aisle of the supermarket. You'll also find tortillas in a variety of flavors such as herb, tomato or spinach, which can be used in Beef Enchiladas Olé.**

Velveeta® Beef Enchiladas Olé

Tacos Olé

1 pound ground beef or turkey
1 cup salsa
¼ cup *Frank's*® *RedHot*® Cayenne Pepper Sauce
2 teaspoons chili powder
8 taco shells, heated
  Garnish: chopped tomatoes, shredded lettuce, sliced olives, sour cream, shredded cheese

1. Cook beef in skillet over medium-high heat 5 minutes or until browned, stirring to separate meat; drain. Stir in salsa, **Frank's RedHot** Sauce and chili powder. Heat to boiling. Reduce heat to medium-low. Cook 5 minutes, stirring often.

2. To serve, spoon meat mixture into taco shells. Splash on more **Frank's RedHot** Sauce to taste. Garnish as desired. *Makes 4 servings*

Prep Time: 5 minutes
Cook Time: 10 minutes

Tacos Olé

Quick Chunky Chili

1 pound lean ground beef
1 medium onion, chopped
1 tablespoon chili powder
1½ teaspoons ground cumin
2 cans (16 ounces each) diced tomatoes, undrained
1 can (15 ounces) pinto beans, drained
½ cup prepared salsa
½ cup (2 ounces) shredded Cheddar cheese
3 tablespoons sour cream
4 teaspoons sliced black olives

Combine meat and onion in 3-quart saucepan; cook over high heat until meat is no longer pink, breaking meat apart with wooden spoon. Add chili powder and cumin; stir 1 minute or until fragrant. Add tomatoes, beans and salsa. Bring to a boil; stir constantly. Reduce heat to low, simmer, covered, 10 minutes. Ladle into bowls. Top with cheese, sour cream and olives.   *Makes 4 (1½-cup) servings*

Serving Suggestion: Serve with tossed green salad and cornbread muffins.

Prep and Cook Time: 25 minutes

Quick Chunky Chili

Pork

Black Bean Sausage Skillet

 2 tablespoons olive oil
 1 cup chopped red onion
 1 cup chopped green bell pepper
 1 pound **BOB EVANS®** Special Seasonings Roll Sausage
 3 (15-ounce) cans black beans, undrained
 1 teaspoon dried oregano leaves
 $\frac{1}{2}$ teaspoon garlic powder
 $\frac{1}{4}$ teaspoon ground cumin
 $\frac{1}{8}$ teaspoon ground cinnamon
   Salt and black pepper to taste
   Cooked rice
   Flour tortillas, cut into wedges (optional)
   Sour cream and salsa for garnish

Heat olive oil in deep skillet; cook and stir onion and bell pepper until tender. Remove from skillet. Crumble sausage into skillet and cook until browned. Drain off any drippings. Return onion and bell pepper to skillet with beans, oregano, garlic, cumin, cinnamon, salt and pepper; simmer 20 minutes. Serve over rice with tortillas, if desired. Garnish with sour cream and salsa. Refrigerate leftovers.

Makes 6 servings

Black Bean Sausage Skillet

Cheese & Chorizo Burritos

Onion-Chili Relish (recipe follows)
24 corn tortillas (4-inch diameter) *or* **6 flour tortillas (8-inch diameter), cut into quarters**
8 ounces queso Chihuahua or Monterey Jack cheese
4 to 6 ounces chorizo
Chilies for garnish

1. Prepare Onion-Chili Relish.

2. Preheat oven to 400°F. Wrap tortillas in foil.

3. Cut cheese into very thin slices. Divide slices evenly among 4 to 6 small, ovenproof plates. (Or, place slices in 1 large, shallow casserole.)

4. Remove and discard casing from chorizo. Heat medium skillet over high heat until hot. Reduce heat to medium. Crumble chorizo into skillet. Brown 6 to 8 minutes; stir to separate meat. Remove with slotted spoon; drain on paper towels. Keep warm.

5. Bake cheese 3 minutes. Place tortillas in oven; continue baking 4 minutes more or until cheese is melted.

6. Place tortillas in serving bowl; sprinkle chorizo evenly over cheese. To serve, spoon cheese mixture onto tortillas and top with relish; fold tortilla around filling. Garnish, if desired.

Makes 4 to 6 servings

Onion-Chili Relish

1 medium white onion, thinly sliced
1 or 2 fresh jalapeño peppers,* stemmed, seeded and thinly sliced
3 tablespoons fresh lime juice
¼ teaspoon salt

*Jalapeño peppers can sting and irritate the skin; wear rubber gloves when handling peppers and do not touch eyes. Wash hands after handling peppers.

Combine all ingredients in small bowl; mix well. Let stand, covered, at room temperature 2 hours to blend flavors.

Makes about 1 cup

Cheese & Chorizo Burritos

Southwestern Ham and Rice

1 (10-ounce) package frozen mixed vegetables
1½ cups sliced fresh mushrooms
½ cup chopped onion
1 tablespoon butter or margarine
1 (11-ounce) can nacho cheese soup
½ cup milk
2 cups (12 ounces) chopped CURE 81® ham
4 cups hot cooked rice

Prepare mixed vegetables according to package directions; drain well. In large skillet over medium-high heat, sauté mushrooms and onion in butter until tender. Stir in soup and milk. Add ham and cooked vegetables. Simmer until thoroughly heated. Serve over rice. *Makes 4 servings*

Chile Relleno Casserole

12 ounces pork sausage
1 small onion, chopped
⅔ cup chunky salsa
¾ cup milk
4 eggs
¼ cup all-purpose flour
½ teaspoon LAWRY'S® Seasoned Pepper
¼ teaspoon LAWRY'S® Garlic Powder with Parsley
2 cups (8 ounces) shredded Monterey Jack cheese
2 cans (7 ounces each) whole green chiles, seeded

In medium skillet, brown pork until crumbly and well done. Add onion and cook over medium-high heat until tender; drain fat. Add salsa; reduce heat to low and cook, uncovered, until mixture thickens. In separate bowl, beat together milk, eggs, flour, Seasoned Pepper and Garlic Powder with Parsley; add cheese. In lightly greased 8×8×2-inch baking dish, layer half chiles, half pork mixture and half cheese-egg mixture; repeat layers. Bake, uncovered, in 350°F. oven 35 minutes. Let stand 10 minutes before serving. *Makes 6 to 8 servings*

Southwestern Ham and Rice

Chunky Ancho Chili with Beans

5 dried ancho chilies
2 cups water
2 tablespoons lard or vegetable oil
1 large onion, chopped
2 cloves garlic, minced
1 pound lean boneless beef, cut into 1-inch cubes
1 pound lean boneless pork, cut into 1-inch cubes
1 to 2 fresh or canned jalapeño peppers,* stemmed, seeded and minced
1 teaspoon salt
1 teaspoon dried oregano
1 teaspoon ground cumin
½ cup dry red wine
3 cups cooked pinto beans _or_ 2 cans (15 ounces each) pinto or kidney beans, drained

*Jalapeño peppers can sting and irritate the skin; wear rubber gloves when handling peppers and do not touch eyes. Wash hands after handling peppers.

Rinse ancho chilies; remove stems, seeds and veins. Place in 2-quart pan with water. Bring to a boil; turn off heat and let stand, covered, 30 minutes or until chilies are soft. Pour chilies with liquid into blender or food processor container fitted with metal blade. Process until smooth; reserve.

Melt lard in 5-quart saucepan over medium heat. Add onion and garlic; cook until onion is tender. Add beef and pork; cook, stirring frequently, until meat is lightly colored. Add jalapeño peppers, salt, oregano, cumin, wine and ancho chili purée. Bring to a boil. Cover; reduce heat and simmer 1½ to 2 hours or until meat is very tender. Stir in beans. Simmer, uncovered, 30 minutes or until chili has thickened slightly. Serve in individual bowls. _Makes 8 servings_

 Señor Says: **To make chili with chili powder, use ⅓ cup chili powder and 1½ cups water in place of ancho chili purée. Reduce salt and cumin to ½ teaspoon each.**

Tostados with Pork

1 pound lean ground pork
1 cup chopped onion
1 jar (8 ounces) taco sauce
1 teaspoon salt
$\frac{1}{2}$ teaspoon chili powder
$\frac{1}{4}$ cup ripe olives, sliced
   Vegetable oil
4 corn or flour tortillas, 7-inch diameter
2 to 4 cups shredded lettuce
$\frac{1}{2}$ cup shredded Monterey Jack or Cheddar cheese (optional)
1 medium tomato, cut into thin wedges
$\frac{1}{2}$ cup sour cream
   Additional taco sauce (optional)

In skillet, lightly brown ground pork with onion; drain any drippings. Add taco sauce, salt and chili powder; cover and cook over low heat 15 minutes or until flavors blend. Stir in ripe olives.

For each tostado, place heated tortilla on plate. Top with layer of lettuce, then hot pork mixture (about $\frac{2}{3}$ cup). Sprinkle with cheese, if desired. Garnish with tomato wedges and dollop of sour cream. Serve with additional taco sauce, if desired.

Makes 4 servings

Prep Time: 25 minutes

*Favorite recipe from **National Pork Board***

Smothered Mexican Pork Chops

1 tablespoon vegetable oil
4 boneless thin-cut pork chops (about ¾ pound)
1 can (14½ ounces) chunky tomatoes, salsa- or Cajun-style
1 can (16 ounces) black beans, drained
2 cups BIRDS EYE® frozen Farm Fresh Mixtures Broccoli, Corn and Red Peppers*

*Or, substitute 2 cups Birds Eye® frozen Corn.

◆ Heat oil in large skillet over high heat. Add pork; cook until browned, about 4 minutes per side.

◆ Add tomatoes; reduce heat to medium. Cover and cook 5 minutes. Uncover and push pork to side of skillet.

◆ Add beans and vegetables. Place pork on top of vegetables. Increase heat to medium-high; cover and cook 5 minutes or until heated through. *Makes about 4 servings*

Prep Time: 5 minutes
Cook Time: 20 minutes

Fantastic Pork Fajitas

1 pound pork strips
2 teaspoons vegetable oil
½ medium onion, peeled and sliced
1 green bell pepper, seeded and sliced
4 flour tortillas, warmed

Heat large nonstick skillet over medium-high heat. Add oil; heat until hot. Add pork strips, onion and bell pepper slices and stir-fry quickly 4 to 5 minutes or until pork is barely pink and vegetables are crisp-tender. Roll up portions of the meat mixture in flour tortillas and serve with purchased salsa, if desired. *Makes 4 servings*

*Favorite recipe from **National Pork Board***

Smothered Mexican Pork Chop

Tacos with Carnitas

2 pound pork leg, shoulder or butt roast, fat trimmed
1 medium onion, peeled, quartered
2 tablespoons chili powder
1 tablespoon dried oregano leaves, crushed
3 bay leaves
1 teaspoon ground cumin
16 (6-inch) corn tortillas
4 cups shredded romaine lettuce
1 cup crumbled feta cheese (optional)
1 can (4 ounces) diced mild green chilies
Salsa Cruda (recipe page 174)

1. Place pork, onion, chili powder, oregano, bay leaves and cumin in large saucepan or Dutch oven. Add enough water to cover pork. Cover and bring to a boil; reduce heat to medium-low. Simmer 3 hours or until meat pulls apart easily when tested with fork.

2. Preheat oven to 450°F. Transfer meat to 9-inch baking pan. Bake 20 minutes or until surface is browned and crisp. Meanwhile, skim fat from cooking liquid. Boil on high heat 20 minutes or until mixture is reduced to about 1 cup. Remove and discard bay leaves.

3. Shred meat by pulling apart with 2 forks. Add meat to reduced cooking liquid; stir to coat completely. Cover; simmer 10 minutes or until meat absorbs most of liquid.

4. Heat large nonstick skillet over medium-high heat. Place 2 inches water in medium bowl. Dip 1 tortilla in water; shake off excess. Place in hot skillet. Cook 30 seconds on each side or until tortilla is hot and pliable but just starting to firm slightly. Transfer to plate and cover to keep warm. Repeat with remaining tortillas.

5. Top each tortilla with ¼ cup lettuce, ¼ cup meat, 1 tablespoon cheese, if desired, 1 teaspoon chilies and 1 tablespoon Salsa Cruda.   *Makes 8 servings*

continued on page 174

Tacos with Carnitas

Salsa Cruda

1 cup chopped tomato
2 tablespoons minced onion
2 tablespoons minced fresh cilantro (optional)
2 tablespoons lime juice
½ jalapeño pepper,* seeded and minced
1 clove garlic, minced

*Jalapeño peppers can sting and irritate the skin; wear rubber gloves when handling peppers and do not touch eyes. Wash hands after handling peppers.

Combine tomato, onion, cilantro, lime juice, jalapeño pepper and garlic in small bowl. Stir to combine.   *Makes about ½ cup*

Fiesta Rice and Sausage

1 teaspoon vegetable oil
2 pounds spicy Italian sausage, casing removed
2 cloves garlic, minced
2 teaspoons ground cumin
4 onions, chopped
4 green bell peppers, chopped
3 jalapeño peppers,* seeded and minced
4 cups beef broth
2 packages (6¼ ounces each) long-grain and wild rice mix

*Jalapeño peppers can sting and irritate the skin; wear rubber gloves when handling peppers and do not touch eyes. Wash hands after handling.

SLOW COOKER DIRECTIONS
Heat oil in large skillet; add sausage. Break up sausage with back of spoon while cooking; cook until browned, about 5 minutes. Add garlic and cumin; cook 30 seconds. Add onions, bell peppers and jalapeño peppers. Sauté mixture until onions are tender, about 10 minutes. Pour mixture into slow cooker. Stir in beef broth and rice.

Cover and cook on HIGH 1 to 2 hours or on LOW 4 to 6 hours.   *Makes 10 to 12 servings*

Tex-Mex Chops

4 boneless pork loin chops, about 1 pound
1 teaspoon vegetable oil
1½ cups bottled salsa, chunky style
1 can (4 ounces) diced green chilies
½ teaspoon ground cumin
¼ cup shredded Cheddar cheese

Heat oil in nonstick pan over medium-high heat. Brown chops on one side, about 2 minutes. Turn chops over. Add salsa, chilies and cumin to skillet; mix well. Lower heat, cover and barely simmer for 8 minutes. Uncover; top each chop with 1 tablespoon cheese. Cover and simmer an additional 2 to 3 minutes or until cheese melts. Serve immediately. *Makes 4 servings*

Prep Time: 15 minutes

Favorite recipe from **National Pork Board**

Baked Pork Fajitas Mexicana

2 medium red or green peppers, cut into strips
1 medium onion, sliced
2 tablespoons oil
1 tablespoon lemon or lime juice
8 boneless pork chops (½ inch thick)
1 envelope SHAKE 'N BAKE® Seasoned Coating Mix Original Pork
Flour tortillas, warmed

MIX peppers, onion, oil and lemon juice in 13×9-inch baking pan until well mixed.

COAT chops with coating mix as directed on package. Place on pepper mixture.

BAKE at 425°F for 20 minutes or until chops are cooked through. Cut chops into slices. Fill tortillas with sliced pork and pepper mixture or serve whole chops and vegetables over rice.
Makes 8 servings

Prep Time: 10 minutes
Bake Time: 20 minutes

Easy Pork Stir-Fry with Peanut Mole

1 tablespoon vegetable oil
½ cup chopped onion
1 pound boneless pork chops, cut into strips
1¼ teaspoons chili powder
1 teaspoon bottled minced garlic
1 teaspoon ground cumin
¼ teaspoon ground red pepper or to taste
1 can (8 ounces) tomato sauce
¼ cup peanut butter
1 tablespoon sugar (optional)
1 tablespoon cornmeal
1 tablespoon unsweetened cocoa powder
¼ cup water
8 corn or flour tortillas (6 or 7 inches)
1 cup shredded lettuce
1 medium tomato, diced

1. Heat oil in large skillet over medium-high heat until hot. Add onion; cook 2 minutes. Add pork, chili powder, garlic, cumin and red pepper. Cook and stir 3 to 4 minutes or until pork is no longer pink in center.

2. Stir in tomato sauce, peanut butter, sugar, if desired, cornmeal, cocoa and water. Reduce heat to medium-low; cook 3 to 4 minutes or until smooth and thickened.

3. Distribute pork evenly over tortillas. Top with lettuce and tomatoes; roll up tortillas.

Makes 4 servings

Tip: Mole (MOH-lay) is a rich, dark brown Mexican sauce made with ground spices, seeds and nuts, onion, garlic and Mexican chocolate. Many American mole recipes use unsweetened cocoa powder and peanut butter as substitutions for the ground nuts and Mexican chocolate.

Prep and Cook Time: 15 minutes

Easy Pork Stir-Fry with Peanut Mole

Carne Adovada

8 to 10 dried red New Mexico or California chilies
2 cups water
⅓ cup finely chopped onion
1 clove garlic, minced
1 teaspoon dried oregano
½ teaspoon salt
½ teaspoon ground cumin
1½ pounds lean boneless pork butt *or* 2 pounds pork chops, cut ½ inch thick

Wash chilies; remove stems and seeds. Place in 3-quart pan with water. Cover and simmer 20 minutes or until chilies are very soft. Pour chilies and liquid into blender or food processor container fitted with metal blade; process until puréed. Push purée through wire strainer; discard pulp. Add onion, garlic, oregano, salt and cumin to chili mixture.

If using pork butt, trim excess fat. Cut meat into ½-inch slices, then cut into strips about 1 inch wide and 3 inches long. If using pork chops, trim fat.

Place meat in heavy resealing plastic food storage bag. Pour chili mixture over meat; seal bag. Refrigerate 1 to 2 days. Preheat oven to 325°F. Transfer meat and chili mixture to 2½-quart casserole; cover. Bake 2 to 2½ hours or until meat is very tender. Skim and discard fat before serving.

Makes 4 to 6 servings

Pork Tenderloin Mole

1½ pounds pork tenderloin (about 2 whole)
1 teaspoon vegetable oil
½ cup chopped onion
1 clove garlic, minced
1 cup Mexican-style chili beans, undrained
¼ cup chili sauce
¼ cup raisins
2 tablespoons water
1 tablespoon peanut butter
1 teaspoon unsweetened cocoa
Dash each salt, ground cinnamon and ground cloves

Place tenderloin in shallow baking pan. Roast at 350°F for 30 minutes or until juicy and slightly pink in center.

Heat oil in medium saucepan. Cook onion and garlic over low heat for 5 minutes. Combine onion and garlic with remaining ingredients in food processor; process until almost smooth. Heat mixture in saucepan thoroughly over low temperature, stirring frequently. Serve over tenderloin slices.

Makes 6 servings

Favorite recipe from **National Pork Board**

Grilled Chili-Marinated Pork

3 tablespoons ground seeded dried pasilla chilies
1 teaspoon coarse or Kosher salt
½ teaspoon ground cumin
2 tablespoons vegetable oil
1 tablespoon fresh lime juice
3 cloves garlic, minced
2 pounds pork tenderloin or thick boneless pork loin chops, trimmed of fat
  Shredded romaine lettuce (optional)
  Radishes for garnish

1. Mix chilies, salt and cumin in small bowl. Stir in oil and lime juice to make smooth paste. Stir in garlic.

2. Butterfly pork by cutting lengthwise about ⅔ of the way through, leaving meat in one piece; spread meat flat. Cut tenderloin crosswise into 8 equal pieces. (If using pork chops, do not cut into pieces.)

3. Place pork between pieces of plastic wrap. Pound with flat side of meat mallet to ¼-inch thickness.

4. Spread chili paste on both sides of pork pieces to coat evenly. Place in shallow glass baking dish. Marinate, covered, in refrigerator 2 to 3 hours.

5. Prepare coals for grill or preheat broiler. Grill or broil pork 6 inches from heat 8 to 10 minutes for grilling or 6 to 7 minutes for broiling, turning once. Serve on lettuce-lined plate. Garnish, if desired.

Makes 6 to 8 servings

Grilled Chili-Marinated Pork

Stir-Fried Pork Burritos

1 pound lean boneless pork loin
2 cloves garlic, minced
1 teaspoon oregano, crumbled
1 teaspoon ground cumin
1 teaspoon seasoned salt
2 tablespoons orange juice
2 tablespoons vinegar
½ teaspoon hot pepper sauce, or to taste
1 tablespoon vegetable oil
1 medium onion, peeled and sliced
1 sweet green bell pepper, seeded and sliced
4 flour tortillas

Slice pork across grain into ⅛-inch strips. Mix together garlic, oregano, cumin, salt, orange juice, vinegar and hot pepper sauce. Marinate pork strips in mixture for 10 minutes. Heat oil in heavy skillet or on griddle until hot. Stir-fry pork strips, onion and bell pepper until pork is no longer pink, about 3 to 5 minutes. Serve with flour tortillas and accompany with sliced green onion, shredded lettuce and salsa, if desired. *Makes 4 servings*

Prep Time: 20 minutes

Favorite recipe from **National Pork Board**

Stir-Fried Pork Burritos

Pork Loin Roasted in Chili-Spice Sauce

1 cup chopped onion
¼ cup orange juice
2 cloves garlic
1 tablespoon cider vinegar
1½ teaspoons chili powder
¼ teaspoon dried thyme leaves
¼ teaspoon ground cumin
¼ teaspoon ground cinnamon
⅛ teaspoon ground allspice
⅛ teaspoon ground cloves
1½ pounds pork loin, fat trimmed
3 firm large bananas
2 limes
1 ripe large papaya, peeled, seeded and cubed
1 green onion, minced

Preheat oven to 350°F. Combine onion, orange juice and garlic in food processor; process until finely chopped. Pour into medium saucepan; stir in vinegar, chili powder, thyme, cumin, cinnamon, allspice and cloves. Simmer over medium-high heat about 5 minutes or until thickened. Cut ¼-inch-deep slits along length of roast from end to end at 1½-inch intervals. Spread about 1 tablespoon spice paste over bottom; place roast in baking pan. Spread remaining 2 tablespoons spice paste over sides and top, working mixture into slits. Cover. Bake 45 minutes or until meat thermometer registers 140°F in center of roast.

Remove roast from oven. *Increase oven temperature to 450°F.* Pour off liquid; discard. Return roast to oven and bake, uncovered, 15 minutes or until spice mixture browns lightly and meat thermometer registers 150°F in center of roast. Remove from oven; tent with foil and let stand 5 minutes before slicing.

Meanwhile, spray 9-inch pie plate or cake pan with nonstick cooking spray. Peel bananas and slice diagonally into ½-inch-thick pieces. Place in pan. Squeeze juice from 1 lime over bananas; toss to coat evenly. Cover; bake in oven while roast stands or until hot. Stir in papaya, juice of remaining lime and green onion. Serve with roast.

Makes 6 servings

Fiesta Pork Chops

4 well-trimmed ¾-inch-thick pork chops
2 teaspoons chili powder
1 tablespoon vegetable oil
1 package (6.8 ounces) RICE-A-RONI® Spanish Rice
2 tablespoons margarine or butter
1 can (14½ ounces) tomatoes, undrained, chopped
½ cup chopped green bell pepper *or* 1 can (4 ounces) chopped green chiles, drained
½ cup chopped onion

1. Evenly sprinkle both sides of pork chops with chili powder. In large skillet, brown pork chops in oil over medium-high heat. Drain; set aside.

2. In same skillet, combine rice-vermicelli mix and margarine. Sauté over medium heat, stirring frequently until vermicelli is golden brown.

3. Stir in 1¾ cups water, Special Seasonings, tomatoes, green pepper and onion; bring to a boil over high heat.

4. Place pork chops over rice mixture; return to a boil. Cover; reduce heat. Simmer 25 to 30 minutes or until liquid is absorbed and rice and chops are tender. *Makes 4 servings*

Southwest Hopping John

1½ cups dried black-eyed peas
2 tablespoons olive oil
1 medium onion, chopped
4 cloves garlic, minced
2 medium red or green bell peppers, chopped
1 jalapeño pepper,* minced
1 teaspoon ground cumin
2½ cups canned chicken broth
1 cup uncooked brown basmati rice
¼ pound smoked ham, diced
4 medium tomatoes, seeded and chopped
½ cup minced fresh cilantro

*Jalapeño peppers can sting and irritate the skin; wear rubber gloves when handling peppers and do not touch eyes. Wash hands after handling.

1. Rinse peas thoroughly in colander under cold running water. Place in large bowl; cover with 4 inches of water. Let stand at least 8 hours, then rinse and drain.

2. Transfer peas to medium saucepan; cover with water. Bring to a boil over high heat. Reduce heat to low; simmer, covered, 1 hour or until tender. Drain in colander; set aside.

3. Heat oil in Dutch oven over medium-high heat. Add onion and garlic; cook and stir 2 minutes. Add bell and jalapeño peppers; cook and stir 2 minutes. Stir in cumin; cook and stir 1 minute.

4. Stir in chicken broth, rice and ham. Bring to a boil over high heat. Reduce heat to low; simmer, covered, 35 minutes.

5. Add peas; simmer 10 minutes or until liquid is absorbed. Stir tomatoes and cilantro into rice mixture just before serving.

Makes 6 servings

Southwest Hopping John

Pork Burritos

2 cups Refried Beans (recipe page 367) or canned refried beans
1 boneless fresh pork butt roast (about 2½ pounds)
1 cup chopped white onion
1 carrot, sliced
1 clove garlic, minced
½ teaspoon salt
½ teaspoon ground cumin
½ teaspoon coriander seeds, lightly crushed
  Water
  Fresh Tomato Salsa (recipe page 190)
12 flour tortillas (8-inch diameter)
2 medium, firm-ripe avocados, pared, pitted, diced
1 cup (4 ounces) shredded Monterey Jack cheese
  Carrot sticks, avocado slices and cilantro sprig for garnish

1. Prepare Refried Beans.

2. Place pork, onion, sliced carrot, garlic, salt, cumin and coriander seeds in 5-quart Dutch oven. Add just enough water to cover pork. Bring to a boil over high heat. Reduce heat to low. Cover and simmer 2 to 2½ hours until pork is tender.

3. Prepare Fresh Tomato Salsa.

4. Preheat oven to 350°F. Remove pork from Dutch oven; set aside. Strain cooking liquid through cheesecloth-lined sieve; reserve ½ cup liquid.

5. Place pork on rack in roasting pan. Roast 40 to 45 minutes until well browned, turning once. Let stand until cool enough to handle.

6. Trim and discard outer fat from pork. Using 2 forks, pull pork into coarse shreds. Combine pork and reserved cooking liquid in medium skillet. Heat over medium heat 5 minutes or until meat is hot and moistly coated with liquid; stir often.

7. Soften and warm tortillas and reheat beans, if necessary. Place about 2½ tablespoons beans on bottom half of 1 tortilla; spread out slightly. Layer with pork, salsa, diced avocado and cheese. Fold right edge of tortilla over filling; fold bottom edge over filling, then loosely roll up, leaving left end of burrito open. Garnish, if desired.   *Makes 6 servings*

continued on page 190

Pork Burritos

Fresh Tomato Salsa

1 medium tomato, finely chopped
¼ cup coarsely chopped fresh cilantro
2 tablespoons finely chopped white onion
1 fresh jalapeño pepper,* seeded and finely chopped
1 tablespoon fresh lime juice

*Jalapeño peppers can sting and irritate the skin; wear rubber gloves when handling peppers and do not touch eyes. Wash hands after handling.

Combine all ingredients in small bowl; mix well. Let stand, covered, at room temperature 1 to 2 hours to blend flavors.   *Makes about ¾ cup*

Roast Pork Tenderloin with Olive and Corn Salsa

2 pounds boneless pork tenderloin
1 to 2 tablespoons *French's*® Worcestershire Sauce
½ cup pitted green olives
½ cup packed fresh parsley
2 tablespoons *Frank's*® *RedHot*® Cayenne Pepper Sauce
2 tablespoons olive oil
2 green onions, cut into 1-inch pieces
1 tablespoon fresh oregano *or* 1 teaspoon dried oregano leaves
1 cup frozen corn, thawed and drained
1 jar (4 ounces) diced pimientos, rinsed and drained

1. Preheat oven to 425°F. Place tenderloin in greased roasting pan. Brush with Worcestershire. Bake 30 to 35 minutes or until center is no longer pink.

2. Combine olives, parsley, **Frank's RedHot** Sauce, oil, onions and oregano in blender or food processor. Cover; process until almost smooth. Transfer to serving bowl; stir in corn and pimientos.

3. Slice tenderloin on the diagonal and serve with salsa.   *Makes 8 servings (1½ cups salsa)*

Prep Time: 20 minutes
Cook Time: 30 minutes

Mexi-Tortilla Casserole

1 tablespoon vegetable oil
1 small onion, chopped
1 pound ground pork
1 can (14½ ounces) diced tomatoes, undrained
1 teaspoon dried oregano, crushed
¼ teaspoon ground cumin
¼ teaspoon salt
¼ teaspoon pepper
1½ cups (6 ounces) shredded Cheddar Jack with jalapeño chilies or taco-style cheese
2 cups tortilla chips
½ cup reduced-fat sour cream
1 can (4 ounces) diced chilies, drained
2 tablespoons minced cilantro

1. Preheat oven to 350°F.

2. Heat oil in large skillet. Add onion and cook 5 minutes or until tender. Add pork and brown, crumbling with a spoon. Pour off fat. Stir in tomatoes, oregano, cumin, salt and pepper. Spoon into 11×7-inch casserole. Sprinkle cheese over casserole; arrange tortilla chips over cheese. Bake casserole 10 to 15 minutes, or until cheese melts.

3. Combine sour cream and chilies; mix until well blended. Drop by tablespoonfuls over baked casserole. Sprinkle with cilantro.   *Makes 6 servings*

Fish & Shellfish

Baked Shrimp with Chili-Garlic Butter

   1½ **pounds medium fresh shrimp in shells**
   ½ **cup butter**
   ¼ **cup vegetable oil**
   8 **cloves garlic, finely chopped**
   1 **to 3 dried de arbol chilies, coarsely crumbled***
   1 **tablespoon fresh lime juice**
   ¼ **teaspoon salt**
      Green onion tops, slivered, for garnish

*For milder flavor, seed some or all of the chilies.

1. Preheat oven to 400°F. Shell and devein shrimp, leaving tails attached; rinse and drain well.

2. Heat butter and oil in small skillet over medium heat until butter is melted and foamy. Add garlic, chilies, lime juice and salt. Cook and stir 1 minute. Remove from heat.

3. Arrange shrimp in even layer in shallow 2-quart gratin pan or baking dish. Pour hot butter mixture over shrimp.

4. Bake shrimp 10 to 12 minutes until shrimp turn pink and opaque, stirring once. Do not overcook or shrimp will be dry and tough. Garnish, if desired. *Makes 4 servings*

Baked Shrimp with Chili-Garlic Butter

Baja Fish Tacos

½ cup sour cream
½ cup mayonnaise
¼ cup chopped fresh cilantro
1 package (1½ ounces) ORTEGA® Taco Seasoning Mix, *divided*
1 pound (about 4) cod or other white fish fillets, cut into 1-inch pieces
2 tablespoons vegetable oil
2 tablespoons lemon juice

Toppings
   Shredded cabbage, chopped tomato, lime juice, ORTEGA® Thick & Smooth Taco Sauce

COMBINE sour cream, mayonnaise, cilantro and 2 tablespoons taco seasoning mix in small bowl.

COMBINE cod, vegetable oil, lemon juice and remaining taco seasoning mix in medium bowl; pour into large skillet. Cook, stirring constantly, over medium-high heat for 4 to 5 minutes or until fish flakes easily when tested with fork.

FILL taco shells with fish mixture. Top with cabbage, tomato, sour cream mixture, lime juice and taco sauce.

Makes 6 servings

Señor Says: **Try a variety of fish and seafood such as shark, shrimp, crab or lobster in these fresh-tasting tacos. Top with desired toppings.**

Baja Fish Tacos

Fillets with Mole Verde

¼ **cup vegetable oil, divided**
¼ **cup chopped white onion**
1 **or** 2 **fresh jalapeño peppers,* seeded and finely chopped**
1 **cup fresh tomatillos, husked,** *or* 1 **can (8 ounces) tomatillos, drained and chopped**
2 **cloves garlic, minced**
¼ **teaspoon ground cumin**
⅓ **cup plus** 1 **tablespoon water, divided**
⅓ **cup coarsely chopped fresh cilantro**
½ **teaspoon salt, divided**
⅓ **cup all-purpose flour**
⅛ **teaspoon black pepper**
1 **egg**
2 **tablespoons butter or margarine**
1½ **to** 2 **pounds small red snapper fillets or skinless sole fillets**
Carrot sticks (optional)
Cilantro sprig and tomatillos for garnish

*Jalapeño peppers can sting and irritate the skin; wear rubber gloves when handling peppers and do not touch eyes. Wash hands after handling.

1. Heat 2 tablespoons oil in small skillet over medium heat until hot. Add onion and jalapeño peppers. Cook and stir 4 minutes or until softened. Add tomatillos, garlic and cumin. Cook and stir 1 minute.

2. Add ⅓ cup water, chopped cilantro and ¼ teaspoon salt. Bring to a boil over high heat. Reduce heat to low. Cover and simmer 20 minutes. Pour into blender; process until smooth. Return sauce to skillet; remove from heat. Set aside.

3. Combine flour, remaining ¼ teaspoon salt and black pepper on plate. Beat egg with remaining 1 tablespoon water in shallow bowl.

4. Heat butter and remaining 2 tablespoons oil in 12-inch skillet over medium-high heat until foamy. Working with as many fillets as will fit in skillet in single layer, lightly coat each fillet on both sides with flour mixture; shake off excess. Dip into egg mixture; let excess drain off. Cook 4 to 8 minutes until light brown on outside and opaque at center, turning once. Remove to serving plate; keep warm. Repeat with remaining fillets.

5. Quickly heat reserved sauce over medium heat until hot, stirring frequently. Pour over and around fish. Serve with carrot sticks and garnish if desired. *Makes 4 to 6 servings*

Fillet with Mole Verde

Time-Out Crab Quesadillas

1 red bell pepper
2 green or yellow bell peppers
1 cup red onion, peeled
  Nonstick cooking spray
2 teaspoons ground cumin
8 flour tortillas
1 tablespoon corn oil
1 cup shredded Monterey Jack cheese
1 cup ($\frac{1}{4}$ pound) well-picked backfin crab (or surimi seafood)
4 jalapeño peppers,* pickled or fresh, seeded and minced
$\frac{1}{4}$ teaspoon salt
3 tablespoons reduced-calorie sour cream
5 tablespoons plain nonfat yogurt

*Jalapeño peppers can sting and irritate the skin; wear rubber gloves when handling peppers and do not touch eyes. Wash hands after handling.

Remove stems and seeds from bell peppers. Cut peppers in half crosswise and cut into thin slivers. Cut onion in half lengthwise. Place onion, cut-side-down, slice into $\frac{1}{8}$-inch thick pieces. Separate pieces.

Spray 10-inch skillet with cooking spray. Heat over medium-high heat 2 minutes. Add bell peppers, onion and cumin. Reduce heat to medium and sauté vegetables until softened.

Brush 1 side of each of flour tortillas with oil and place, oiled-side-down, on plate. Sprinkle 2 tablespoons cheese over each tortilla, leaving 1-inch border around edge. Spoon $\frac{1}{4}$ each of the cooked peppers and crab over cheese; sprinkle with jalapeño peppers to taste, 2 tablespoons of cheese and salt. Moisten edges of the filled tortilla and of a second tortilla with water. Place tortillas together and firmly press edges to seal. (Don't worry if some of edge remains open.) Lightly brush top of tortilla with oil and cover with plastic wrap.

Heat same skillet over medium heat. Slide quesadilla into pan and sauté 3 to 4 minutes or until golden brown, pressing top with spatula. Flip quesadilla and brown second side about 4 minutes. Cut quesadilla into 6 wedges, loosely wrap in foil and keep warm in 225°F oven while cooking remaining quesadillas, if desired. Mix sour cream and yogurt in small bowl. Serve with warm quesadillas.

Makes 24 wedges

Favorite recipe from **National Fisheries Institute**

Shrimp with Chile Cilantro Rice

4 cups cooked long-grain white rice
1 cup Green Chile-Cilantro Pesto (recipe follows)
½ cup chicken broth
4 slices (about 4 ounces) bacon
1 pound (uncooked) large or medium shrimp, peeled and deveined
½ cup (about 4) chopped green onions
2 cloves garlic, finely chopped
ORTEGA® Salsa Prima-Thick & Chunky Mild

COMBINE rice, Green Chile-Cilantro Pesto and broth in medium saucepan; cook over medium heat until heated through. Keep warm.

COOK bacon in large skillet over medium-high heat until crisp. Crumble bacon; set aside. Discard all but 2 tablespoons drippings from skillet. Add shrimp, green onions and garlic; cook, stirring frequently, for 3 to 5 minutes or until shrimp turn pink.

PLACE rice mixture on platter; top with shrimp mixture, salsa and bacon.   *Makes 6 to 8 servings*

Green Chile-Cilantro Pesto: **COMBINE** 2 cups fresh cilantro sprigs, 1 cup (7-ounce can) ORTEGA® Diced Green Chiles, 1 cup (4 ounces) grated Parmesan cheese, ¾ cup toasted pine nuts, 4 large cloves peeled garlic and 1 tablespoon lime juice in food processor or blender; cover. Process until well chopped. Process, while slowly adding ½ cup corn oil, for additional 20 to 30 seconds or until mixture is almost smooth.

Fish Veracruz

Fish

   8 (about 1½ pounds *total*) red snapper or halibut fillets
½ cup (about 4 limes) lime juice
½ teaspoon salt (optional)

Sauce

   2 tablespoons vegetable oil
1 cup (1 small) onion slices
1 cup (1 small) green bell pepper strips
3 cloves garlic, finely chopped
⅓ cup dry white wine or chicken broth
1¾ cups (16-ounce jar) ORTEGA® Salsa Prima-Thick & Chunky Mild
½ cup tomato sauce
¼ cup ORTEGA® Sliced Jalapeños
¼ cup sliced ripe olives
1 tablespoon capers (such as CROSSE & BLACKWELL®)
Fresh cilantro sprigs (optional)
Lime wedges (optional)

FOR FISH
ARRANGE fish in 13×9-inch baking pan. Sprinkle with lime juice and salt, if desired. Cover; refrigerate for at least 20 minutes.

FOR SAUCE
HEAT vegetable oil in large, nonstick skillet over medium-high heat. Add onion, bell pepper and garlic; cook for 1 to 2 minutes or until vegetables are crisp-tender. Add wine; cook for 1 minute.

STIR in salsa, tomato sauce, jalapeños, olives and capers. Bring to a boil. Place fish in sauce. Reduce heat to low. Cook, covered, for 8 to 10 minutes or until fish flakes when tested with fork. Serve with cilantro and lime.

Makes 8 servings

Fish Veracruz

Scallop and Yellow Rice Salad

2 jalapeño or serrano peppers,* seeded
1 clove garlic, peeled
⅓ cup plus 2 tablespoons vegetable oil, divided
½ cup chopped onion
2 cups water
½ teaspoon ground turmeric
½ teaspoon ground cumin
½ teaspoon salt
1 cup uncooked long-grain white rice
1 pound bay scallops or quartered sea scallops
1 can (15 ounces) black beans, rinsed and drained
1 cup chopped tomatoes
¼ cup chopped fresh cilantro or parsley
3 tablespoons lime juice
Lime wedges and grated lime peel for garnish

*Jalapeño and other chili peppers can sting and irritate the skin; wear rubber gloves when handling peppers and do not touch eyes. Wash hands after handling.

1. Combine jalapeño peppers and garlic in food processor or blender. Process until finely minced.

2. Heat 2 tablespoons oil in large saucepan over medium heat. Add onion and jalapeño pepper mixture. Cook and stir 3 to 4 minutes or until onion is softened. Add water, turmeric, cumin and salt. Bring mixture to a boil over high heat; add rice. Cover; reduce heat to low. Simmer 15 to 20 minutes or until most of the liquid is absorbed.

3. Stir in scallops; cover. Simmer 2 to 3 minutes or until scallops turn opaque and are cooked through.

4. Transfer rice mixture to large bowl; set bowl in ice water to chill rice and prevent scallops from overcooking.

5. Toss mixture every few minutes. When mixture is lukewarm, stir in beans, tomatoes and cilantro.

6. Combine remaining ⅓ cup oil and lime juice in 1-cup glass measure. Pour over salad and toss. Serve immediately or refrigerate and serve chilled. Garnish just before serving.   *Makes 5 servings*

Scallop and Yellow Rice Salad

Red Snapper in Chili-Tomato Sauce

6 red snapper fillets (8 to 10 ounces each)
¼ teaspoon salt
⅛ teaspoon black pepper
⅓ cup all-purpose flour
¼ cup olive oil
3 cloves garlic, sliced
2 medium white onions, cut lengthwise into thin slivers
1½ pounds fresh plum tomatoes, peeled, seeded and finely chopped
½ cup tomato juice
¼ cup fresh lime juice
¼ cup sliced pimiento-stuffed green olives
1 or 2 pickled jalapeño peppers,* seeded and finely chopped
1 tablespoon drained capers
1 bay leaf
Fresh bay leaves and lime slices for garnish
Boiled, quartered new potatoes with fresh dill (optional)

*Jalapeño peppers can sting and irritate the skin; wear rubber gloves when handling peppers and do not touch eyes. Wash hands after handling.

1. Sprinkle fish with salt and black pepper. Coat both sides of fish with flour; shake off excess.

2. Heat oil in 12-inch skillet over medium heat. Add garlic; cook and stir 2 to 3 minutes until golden. Remove garlic with slotted spoon; discard.

3. Place fillets in single layer in skillet without crowding. Cook over medium heat 4 minutes or until fillets are light brown, turning once. Remove to plate. Repeat with remaining fillets.

4. Add onions. Cook and stir 4 minutes or until onions are softened. Stir in tomatoes, tomato juice, lime juice, olives, jalapeño peppers, capers and bay leaf. Bring to a boil over high heat. Reduce heat to low. Cover and simmer 15 minutes.

5. Add any accumulated juices from fillets on plate to skillet. Increase heat to medium-high. Cook, uncovered, 2 to 3 minutes until thickened, stirring frequently. Remove and discard bay leaf.

6. Return fillets to skillet. Spoon sauce over fillets. Reduce heat to low. Cover; simmer 3 to 5 minutes until fillets flake easily when tested with a fork. Garnish, if desired. Serve with potatoes, if desired.

Makes 6 servings

Red Snapper in Chili-Tomato Sauce

Fish Burritos

WESSON® No-Stick Cooking Spray
1 cup diced onion
1 pound orange roughy fillets or any white fish fillets
3 limes
1 (16-ounce) can ROSARITA® No Fat Traditional Refried Beans
8 burrito-size fat-free flour tortillas
2 cups cooked white rice
1½ cups shredded cabbage
¾ cup reduced-fat shredded sharp Cheddar cheese
¾ cup diced tomatoes
ROSARITA® Traditional Mild Salsa

1. Spray large no-stick skillet with Wesson Cooking Spray. Sauté onion until tender.

2. Add fish and juice from 1 lime. Cook until fish becomes flakey; shred with fork. Remove from heat. Set aside.

3. Evenly divide Rosarita Beans among *each* tortilla; spread beans down center of tortillas. Top beans with even amounts of fish, rice, cabbage, cheese and tomatoes.

4. Roll burrito-style, folding in edges. Serve with Rosarita Salsa and lime wedges.

Makes 8 burritos

Mexican Stir-Fry

1 pound halibut steaks
⅓ cup bottled picante sauce
2 tablespoons lime juice
¼ cup chicken broth
1½ teaspoons cornstarch
¼ teaspoon chili powder
1 tablespoon vegetable oil
12 cherry tomatoes, halved
1 cup frozen corn, thawed
1 can (15 ounces) black beans, rinsed and drained
2 tablespoons cilantro, minced

Trim skin from halibut; cut into bite-sized pieces. Combine halibut, picante sauce and lime juice in large non-metallic bowl. Stir well; cover and refrigerate 30 minutes.

Combine chicken broth, cornstarch and chili powder in medium bowl; set aside. Drain halibut. Heat oil in nonstick wok or skillet; add halibut and stir-fry 1½ minutes. Add tomatoes, corn, beans and cilantro. Stir in broth mixture. Cover and cook, stirring occasionally until thickened. Serve over rice with additional picante sauce, if desired. *Makes 4 servings*

Favorite recipe from **National Fisheries Institute**

Tuna Quesadilla Stack

4 (10-inch) flour tortillas, divided
1/4 cup plus 2 tablespoons pinto or black bean dip
1 can (9 ounces) tuna packed in water, drained and flaked
2 cups (8 ounces) shredded Cheddar cheese
1 can (14 1/2 ounces) diced tomatoes, drained
1/2 cup thinly sliced green onions
1 1/2 teaspoons butter or margarine, melted

1. Preheat oven to 400°F.

2. Place 1 tortilla on 12-inch pizza pan. Spread with 2 tablespoons bean dip, leaving 1/2-inch border. Top with one third each of tuna, cheese, tomatoes and green onions. Repeat layers twice beginning with tortilla and ending with onions.

3. Top with remaining tortilla, pressing gently. Brush with melted butter.

4. Bake 15 minutes or until cheese melts and top is lightly browned. Cool and cut into 8 wedges.

Makes 4 servings

Tip: For a special touch, serve with assorted toppings, such as guacamole, sour cream and salsa.

Prep and Cook Time: 25 minutes

Baked Fish Steaks

1 tablespoon annatto seeds
1 cup boiling water
1 tablespoon plus 1½ teaspoons orange juice
1 tablespoon plus 1½ teaspoons cider vinegar
2 cloves garlic, chopped
1 small dried de arbol chili, coarsely crumbled
¾ teaspoon ground cumin
½ teaspoon ground allspice
¼ teaspoon salt
⅛ teaspoon black pepper
4 pieces fresh halibut steaks, mackerel or sea bass fillets (about 8 ounces each)
  Vegetable oil
  Sliced green onions
  Orange peel for garnish

1. Place annatto seeds in small bowl; cover with boiling water. Let stand, covered, at room temperature at least 8 hours or overnight.

2. Drain annatto seeds; discard liquid. Place annatto seeds, orange juice, vinegar, garlic, chili, cumin, allspice, salt and pepper in blender; process until smooth.

3. Spread annatto paste over both sides of fish to coat. Arrange fish in single layer in well-oiled baking dish. Cover and refrigerate 1 to 2 hours to blend flavors.

4. Preheat oven to 350°F. Bake fish, uncovered, 20 to 25 minutes until fish flakes easily when tested with fork. Sprinkle green onions over tops before serving. Garnish as desired.   *Makes 4 servings*

Baked Fish Steak

Shrimp and Black Bean Wraps

4 large flour tortillas
1 tablespoon olive oil
8 ounces small shrimp, peeled and deveined
1 (15-ounce) can black beans, drained
1 large tomato, chopped
2 green onions, sliced
1½ teaspoons TABASCO® brand Pepper Sauce
½ teaspoon salt

Preheat oven to 375°F. Wrap tortillas in foil; place in oven 10 minutes to warm. Heat oil in 10-inch skillet over medium-high heat. Add shrimp; cook and stir until pink. Mash ½ cup beans in medium bowl; stir in remaining beans, shrimp, tomato, green onions, TABASCO® Sauce and salt. To assemble, place ¼ of mixture on each tortilla; roll up tortillas, tucking in sides. Slice in half, if desired.

Makes 4 servings

Pescado Borracho

1½ pounds red snapper fillets
   All-purpose flour
4 tablespoons vegetable oil, divided
1 small onion, chopped
1 can (14½ ounces) whole peeled tomatoes, undrained and cut up
1 package (1.0 ounce) LAWRY'S® Taco Spices & Seasonings
2 tablespoons diced green chiles
½ cup dry red wine

Dip fish in flour to coat. In large skillet, heat 2 tablespoons oil. Add fish and cook over medium-high heat until browned. In 2-quart oblong baking dish, place browned fish; set aside. Add remaining 2 tablespoons oil and onion to skillet; cook onion about 5 minutes or until tender. Add remaining ingredients except wine. Bring to a boil over medium-high heat, stirring constantly; add wine and mix well. Pour tomato mixture over fish. Bake, uncovered, in 400°F oven 15 to 20 minutes or until fish flakes easily with fork.

Makes 4 to 6 servings

Serving Suggestion: Serve each fillet with sauce; garnish with parsley.

Shrimp and Black Bean Wrap

Surimi Seafood with Black Beans and Cilantro Sauce

Cilantro Sauce (recipe page 215)

2 cups frozen corn

1 can (16 ounces) black beans, rinsed and drained well

¼ cup chopped red bell pepper

1 can (4 ounces) chopped green chilies, drained

¼ cup minced fresh cilantro

4 green onions with tops, minced

12 ounces lobster-flavored surimi seafood chunks, shredded or flake style

2 cloves garlic, minced

1 teaspoon ground cumin

¼ teaspoon freshly ground black pepper

2 tablespoons white wine vinegar

2 tablespoons water

2 teaspoons fresh lime juice

3 tablespoons olive oil

½ teaspoon minced jalapeño pepper (optional)

Prepare Cilantro Sauce; set aside. Place corn in fine mesh strainer; rinse with cold water to thaw. Drain well. In large bowl, combine corn, beans, red pepper, chilies, cilantro, green onions and surimi seafood. On cutting board, with point of sharp knife, mash garlic, cumin and black pepper to form paste. Place paste in small bowl; whisk in vinegar, water and lime juice. Gradually whisk in oil. Drizzle vinaigrette over bean mixture and toss.

Serve salad at room temperature in individual bowls or lettuce cups. If chilling salad, taste and adjust seasonings before serving. Pass Cilantro Sauce separately. Garnish with jalapeño pepper, if desired.

Makes 4 servings

Cilantro Sauce

> 1 cup plain nonfat yogurt
> ¼ cup minced cilantro
> ½ teaspoon sugar
> ¼ teaspoon salt
> ⅛ to ¼ teaspoon ground red pepper

Combine ingredients in small bowl.

Makes 1½ cups

*Favorite recipe from **National Fisheries Institute***

Salsa Shrimp and Rice

> 1 tablespoon olive oil
> ¼ cup chopped onion
> 1 clove garlic, minced
> 1 cup prepared green salsa
> ¾ cup white wine
> 1 tablespoon lemon juice
> 12 ounces medium shrimp, peeled and deveined
> 4 cups hot cooked white rice

Heat large nonstick skillet over medium-high heat; add oil and heat until hot. Add onion; cook and stir until onion is translucent. Add garlic; cook and stir 1 minute. Add salsa, wine and lemon juice; bring to a boil. Reduce heat to medium-low; simmer 10 minutes. Add shrimp; cook about 2 minutes or until shrimp turn pink and opaque, stirring occasionally. Serve shrimp mixture over rice. Garnish as desired.

Makes 4 servings

Lime-Poached Fish with Corn and Chili Salsa

4 swordfish steaks, 1 inch thick (about 1½ pounds)*
1 cup baby carrots, cut lengthwise into halves
2 green onions, cut into 1-inch pieces
3 tablespoons lime juice
½ teaspoon salt, divided
½ teaspoon chili powder
1½ cups chopped tomatoes
1 cup frozen corn, thawed
1 can (4 ounces) chopped green chilies, drained
2 tablespoons chopped fresh cilantro
1 tablespoon margarine or butter

*Tuna or halibut steaks can be substituted.

1. Place fish and carrots in saucepan just large enough to hold them in 1 layer. Add onions, lime juice, ¼ teaspoon salt and chili powder. Add enough water to just cover fish.

2. Bring to a simmer over medium heat. Cook 8 minutes or until center of fish begins to flake easily when tested with fork. Transfer to serving plates with spatula.

3. While fish is cooking, prepare salsa. Combine tomatoes, corn, chilies, cilantro and remaining ¼ teaspoon salt in medium bowl; toss well.

4. Drain carrots; add margarine. Transfer to serving plates; serve with salsa.   *Makes 4 servings*

Tip: If time allows, prepare the salsa in advance so the flavors have more time to develop. Do not add salt until ready to serve. Cover and refrigerate salsa up to 1 day before serving.

Prep and Cook Time: 15 minutes

Lime-Poached Fish with Corn and
Chili Salsa

Clams Picante

16 cherrystone clams,* scrubbed and soaked
1 can (16 ounces) whole kernel corn, drained
2 cups peeled, seeded and chopped cucumbers
1 cup chopped tomatoes
1 can (4 ounces) diced green chilies
¼ cup chopped onion
2 tablespoons lime juice
1 tablespoon chopped fresh cilantro
   Tortilla chips or soft flour tortillas (optional)

*If fresh clams in shells are not available, substitute ¾ to 1 cup shucked clams. Steam in vegetable steamer until firm. Chop clams. Omit step 1.

1. Place 1 cup water in large stockpot. Bring to a boil over high heat. Add clams. Cover and reduce heat to medium. Steam 5 to 7 minutes or until clams open. Remove clams as they open. (Discard any clams that remain unopened.) Remove clams from shells and chop.

2. Combine clams, corn, cucumbers, tomatoes, chilies, onion, lime juice and cilantro in glass bowl. Cover and refrigerate several hours or overnight to allow flavors to blend. Serve with tortilla chips, if desired.

Makes about 4 cups

Clams Picante

Shrimp Enchiladas

    1 jar (26 to 28 ounces) RAGÚ® Old World Style® Pasta Sauce
    1 can (4 ounces) chopped green chilies, drained
1½ tablespoons chili powder
    1 pound cooked shrimp, coarsely chopped
    2 cups shredded Monterey Jack cheese (about 8 ounces)
    1 container (8 ounces) sour cream
    1 package (8 ounces) corn tortillas (12 tortillas), softened

1. Preheat oven to 400°F. In medium bowl, combine Ragú Pasta Sauce, chilies and chili powder. Evenly spread 1 cup sauce mixture in 13×9-inch baking dish; set aside.

2. In another medium bowl, combine shrimp, 1 cup cheese and sour cream. Evenly spread mixture onto tortillas; roll up. Arrange seam side down in prepared dish and top with remaining sauce mixture. Cover with aluminum foil and bake 20 minutes.

3. Remove foil and sprinkle with remaining 1 cup cheese. Bake an additional 5 minutes or until cheese is melted. *Makes 6 servings*

Prep Time: 10 minutes
Cook Time: 40 minutes

Señor Says: **To soften tortillas, arrange on a microwave-safe plate, cover with a dampened paper towel and microwave at HIGH 30 seconds.**

Southwest Tuna Sandwiches

2 cans (6 ounces each) tuna in water, drained
1 can (4 ounces) chopped mild green chilies
½ cup reduced-fat mayonnaise
½ cup finely chopped seeded peeled cucumber
½ cup chopped red bell pepper
¼ cup chopped green onions
¼ cup finely chopped fresh cilantro
½ teaspoon cumin
¼ teaspoon garlic powder
Salt and pepper to taste
4 small pita breads (6-inch size)
1 cup shredded leaf lettuce
½ cup sliced pitted black olives
½ cup chopped tomatoes
½ cup (2 ounces) shredded Cheddar cheese

Combine tuna, chilies, mayonnaise, cucumber, bell pepper, green onions, cilantro, cumin and garlic powder in medium bowl. Toss to mix. Break up large chunks of tuna; do not flake finely. Add salt and pepper to taste. Cover and refrigerate 1 hour or until chilled.

Cut each pita in half crosswise and fill with tuna salad. Add lettuce, olives, tomatoes and Cheddar cheese to each pita half and serve. *Makes 4 servings*

Grilled Salmon Quesadillas with Cucumber Salsa

1 medium cucumber, peeled, seeded and finely chopped
½ cup green or red salsa
1 (8-ounce) salmon fillet
3 tablespoons olive oil, divided
4 (10-inch) flour tortillas, warmed
6 ounces goat cheese, crumbled *or* 1½ cups (6 ounces) shredded Monterey Jack cheese
¼ cup drained sliced pickled jalapeño peppers*

*Jalapeño peppers can sting and irritate the skin; wear rubber gloves when handling peppers and do not touch eyes. Wash hands after handling.

1. Prepare grill for direct cooking. Combine cucumber and salsa in small bowl; set aside.

2. Brush salmon with 2 tablespoons oil. Grill, covered, over medium-hot coals 5 to 6 minutes per side or until fish flakes easily when tested with fork. Transfer to plate; flake with fork.

3. Spoon salmon evenly over half of each tortilla, leaving 1-inch border. Sprinkle with cheese and jalapeño pepper slices. Fold tortillas in half. Brush tortillas with remaining 1 tablespoon oil.

4. Grill quesadillas over medium-hot coals until browned on both sides and cheese is melted. Serve with cucumber salsa. *Makes 4 servings*

Prep and Cook Time: 20 minutes

Grilled Salmon Quesadilla with
Cucumber Salsa

Southwestern Scallops

1 pound bay scallops or 1 pound sea scallops, cut into quarters
½ cup lime juice
⅓ cup olive oil
1 teaspoon grated lime peel
1 green onion with top, sliced diagonally into ½-inch pieces
2 tablespoons chopped fresh cilantro
1 tablespoon chopped fresh parsley
  Salt
  Black pepper
½ cup Italian-style roasted peppers, cut into thin strips
1 avocado
  Lime juice
1 medium tomato, coarsely chopped
1 medium tomato, thinly sliced and cut into halves

Bring 3 inches salted water in large saucepan over high heat to a boil. Reduce heat to low. Add scallops; poach 1 minute. Immediately drain and rinse with cold water. Whisk ½ cup lime juice, oil and lime peel in medium bowl until combined. Stir in scallops, onion, cilantro and parsley. Season to taste with salt and black pepper. Stir in roasted peppers. Refrigerate, covered, 1 hour or until chilled. To serve, slice avocado; toss with lime juice. Add avocado and chopped tomato to scallop mixture. Spoon into serving plate. Arrange tomato slices around edge of plate. *Makes 6 servings*

Southwestern Scallops

Meatless Meals

Rice, Cheese & Bean Enchiladas

    1 (2-cup) bag UNCLE BEN'S® Boil-in-Bag Rice
    4 cups shredded zucchini, drained (2 medium)
    1 tablespoon reduced-sodium taco sauce mix
    1 can (15 ounces) pinto beans, rinsed and drained
    1 can (10 ounces) reduced-fat, reduced-sodium cream of mushroom soup
    1 can (8 ounces) diced green chilies
   12 (8-inch) flour tortillas
    2 cups (8 ounces) reduced-fat Mexican cheese blend, divided

1. Prepare rice following package directions.

2. Combine zucchini and 1 tablespoon taco sauce mix in large nonstick skillet. Cook and stir zucchini 5 minutes. Add beans, soup, chilies and rice. Bring to a boil.

3. Spray 13×9-inch microwavable baking dish with nonstick cooking spray. Spoon about ½ cup of rice mixture onto center of each tortilla. Top with 2 tablespoons cheese. Roll up to enclose filling; place in baking dish. Sprinkle remaining cheese over enchiladas. Microwave at HIGH 4 minutes or until cheese is melted.   *Makes 6 servings*

Serving Suggestion: Serve with sliced mango or orange sections.

Rice, Cheese & Bean Enchilada

South-of-the-Border Lunch Express

½ cup chopped tomato
¼ cup chunky salsa
¼ cup drained and rinsed black beans
¼ cup frozen whole kernel corn, thawed
1 teaspoon chopped fresh cilantro
¼ teaspoon bottled chopped garlic
   Dash ground red pepper
1 cup cooked brown rice
   Reduced-fat Cheddar cheese (optional)

1. Combine tomato, salsa, beans, corn, cilantro, garlic and red pepper in 1-quart microwavable bowl. Cover with vented plastic wrap. Microwave at HIGH 1 to 1½ minutes or until heated through; stir.

2. Microwave rice at HIGH 1 to 1½ minutes in 1-quart microwavable dish or until heated through. Top with tomato mixture and cheese, if desired.   *Makes 1 serving*

Chilaquiles

2 tablespoons vegetable oil
1 medium onion, chopped
1 can (1 pound 12 ounces) whole tomatoes, cut up
1 can (4 ounces) diced green chiles (optional)
1 package (1.0 ounce) LAWRY'S® Taco Spices & Seasonings
6 ounces tortilla chips
4 cups (16 ounces) shredded Monterey Jack cheese
1 cup sour cream
½ cup (2 ounces) shredded cheddar cheese

In large skillet, heat oil. Add onion and cook over medium-high heat until tender. Add tomatoes, chiles and Taco Spices & Seasonings; mix well. Simmer over low heat, uncovered, 10 to 15 minutes. In lightly greased 2-quart casserole, layer ½ of tortilla chips, sauce and Monterey Jack cheese. Repeat layers; top with sour cream. Bake in 350°F oven 30 minutes. Sprinkle with cheddar cheese and bake 10 minutes longer. Let stand 15 minutes before cutting into squares.   *Makes 6 to 8 servings*

South-of-the-Border Lunch Express

Mexican-Style Stuffed Peppers

6 medium red or green bell peppers, halved, seeded
3 tablespoons water
2 cups cooked long-grain white rice
1¾ cups (1-pound jar) ORTEGA® Salsa Prima-Garden Style Mild, *divided*
1½ cups (6 ounces) shredded Cheddar cheese, *divided*
¾ cup frozen peas and carrots
¾ cup whole-kernel corn
½ cup (about 3) chopped green onions
½ teaspoon garlic salt

PREHEAT oven to 375°F.

PLACE bell peppers and water in microwave-safe dish; cover with plastic wrap. Microwave on HIGH (100%) power for 4 to 5 minutes or until slightly tender; drain.

COMBINE rice, *¾ cup* salsa, *1 cup* cheese, peas and carrots, corn, green onions and garlic salt in large bowl. Fill peppers with mixture, mounding slightly. Place peppers in ungreased 13×9-inch baking pan; top with *remaining 1 cup* salsa and *remaining ½ cup* cheese. Cover.

BAKE for 35 to 40 minutes. Uncover; bake for additional 5 minutes or until heated through and cheese is melted.

Makes 6 servings

For Freeze Ahead: **PREPARE** as above; do not bake. Cover; freeze for up to 2 months. Thaw overnight in refrigerator. **PREHEAT** oven to 375°F. **BAKE** for 40 to 45 minutes. Uncover, bake for additional 5 minutes or until heated through and cheese is melted.

Mexican-Style Stuffed Pepper

Meatless Meals   231

Sweet Bean of Youth Tostada

8 (6- to 7-inch) corn tortillas
  Olive oil cooking spray
2 (15½- to 19-ounce) cans black beans, undrained
2 tablespoons olive oil
1 (16-ounce) jar NEWMAN'S OWN® Pineapple Salsa
2 ripe plum tomatoes, diced
1 medium avocado, diced
1 medium mango, diced
½ medium jicama, diced
2 tablespoons NEWMAN'S OWN® Light Italian Salad Dressing
2 tablespoons fresh lime juice
4 ounces queso fresco (Mexican or basket cheese), crumbled, or Monterey Jack cheese, shredded
½ cup loosely packed fresh cilantro leaves, chopped
¼ cup roasted pumpkin seeds, chopped

Preheat oven to 350°F. Spray tortillas on both sides with olive oil spray and toast in oven until crisp, about 10 minutes. Set aside.

In 10-inch nonstick skillet over medium-high heat, sauté black beans, with ¼ cup of their juice, in olive oil 15 minutes, mashing with back of spoon. Add salsa and cook 5 minutes.

Toss tomatoes, avocado, mango and jicama with salad dressing and lime juice. Mix cheese with cilantro and pumpkin seeds.

Spread tortillas with thick layer of bean mixture, spoon fruit salad on top and sprinkle generously with cheese mixture.

Serve immediately.   *Makes 4 servings*

Bean Patties with Picante

2 cups KELLOGG'S® RICE KRISPIES® cereal, divided
1 can (15.5 ounces) pinto beans
2 tablespoons finely chopped onion
2 tablespoons finely chopped sweet red pepper
2 teaspoons finely chopped, seeded jalapeño pepper*
1 tablespoon chopped cilantro
¼ teaspoon garlic salt
¼ teaspoon cumin
¾ cup medium picante sauce

*Jalapeño peppers can sting and irritate the skin. Wear rubber gloves when handling peppers and do not touch eyes. Wash hands after handling.

1. Crush ½ cup of the Kellogg's® Rice Krispies® cereal into fine crumbs. Set aside.

2. Drain beans, reserving liquid. Place beans, ¼ cup bean liquid and remaining cereal in large mixing bowl. Coarsely mash with potato masher or pastry blender. Stir in onion, red pepper, jalapeño pepper, cilantro, garlic salt and cumin. Using ⅓ cup measure, portion mixture and shape into 6 patties. Coat with crushed cereal.

3. Heat large nonstick skillet over medium heat or electric skillet at 325°F. Coat with cooking spray. Place patties in hot skillet and cook for 5 minutes on each side or until golden brown. Serve hot with picante sauce. *Makes 6 servings*

Prep Time: 20 minutes
Cook Time: 10 minutes

Zesty Zucchini Burritos

6 (6-inch) flour tortillas
2 teaspoons olive oil
1 medium zucchini, chopped
¼ cup chopped onion
¾ cup prepared pinto bean dip
¼ cup prepared green salsa
1 tablespoon chopped fresh cilantro
2 cups shredded romaine lettuce
1 cup prepared tomato salsa

Preheat oven to 350°F. Wrap tortillas in foil; place on center rack of oven. Heat 10 minutes or until warm. Meanwhile, heat oil in large skillet over medium-high heat until hot. Add zucchini and onion. Cook and stir until zucchini is crisp-tender; stir in bean dip, green salsa and cilantro.

Divide lettuce evenly among 6 plates. Spoon zucchini mixture evenly onto tortillas. Roll up tortillas; place on lettuce. Top with tomato salsa. Garnish as desired. *Makes 6 servings*

Zesty Zucchini Burrito

Vegetarian Chili

    1 tablespoon vegetable oil
    2 cloves garlic, finely chopped
1½ cups thinly sliced mushrooms
⅔ cup chopped red onion
⅔ cup chopped red bell pepper
    2 teaspoons chili powder
¼ teaspoon ground cumin
⅛ teaspoon ground red pepper (optional)
⅛ teaspoon dried oregano leaves
    1 can (28 ounces) peeled whole tomatoes
⅔ cup frozen baby lima beans
½ cup rinsed and drained canned Great Northern beans
    4 tablespoons nonfat sour cream
    4 tablespoons shredded reduced-fat Cheddar cheese

1. Heat oil in large nonstick saucepan over medium-high heat until hot. Add garlic. Cook and stir 3 minutes. Add mushrooms, onion and bell pepper. Cook 5 minutes, stirring occasionally. Add chili powder, cumin, red pepper, if desired, and oregano. Cook and stir 1 minute. Add tomatoes and beans. Reduce heat to medium-low. Simmer 15 minutes, stirring occasionally.

2. Serve with sour cream and cheese.   *Makes 4 servings*

Vegetarian Chili

Stuffed Chayotes

2 large chayotes, cut in half lengthwise
  Boiling water
2 tablespoons butter or margarine
½ cup chopped onion
1 clove garlic, minced
1 large tomato, peeled, seeded and chopped
2 tablespoons chopped fresh parsley
½ cup cooked whole kernel corn
½ teaspoon salt
⅛ teaspoon black pepper
½ cup (2 ounces) shredded Cheddar cheese

Cook chayote halves in 1 inch boiling water in large covered skillet 20 to 25 minutes or until tender; drain. When cool, remove pulp, leaving ½-inch shells; coarsely chop pulp and edible seeds. Melt butter in large skillet over medium heat. Brush half of the butter inside chayote shells. Add onion and garlic to remaining butter in skillet; cook until onion is tender. Add tomato and parsley; simmer 5 minutes or until liquid has evaporated. Remove from heat; stir in corn, salt, pepper and chayote pulp.

Preheat oven to 375°F. Place chayote shells in greased shallow baking pan. Evenly fill shells with corn mixture; top with cheese. Bake, uncovered, 15 minutes or until chayotes are hot and cheese is melted.

Makes 4 servings

Stuffed Summer Squash: Follow directions for Stuffed Chayotes but use 8 large pattypan squash or 8 zucchini (each about 6 inches long) in place of chayotes. Boil whole squash 8 to 10 minutes or until barely tender. After scooping out pulp, turn shells upside down on paper towels to drain before filling. Makes 8 servings.

Stuffed Chayotes

Onion and Roasted Pepper Tamale Pie with Salsa Colorado

2½ cups all-purpose flour
1 cup masa harina de maiz*
½ teaspoon salt
½ pound butter, chilled and cut into bits
8 to 10 tablespoons ice water
3 medium onions, thinly sliced
1 tablespoon olive oil
2 (4-ounce) cans whole green chiles, drained, patted dry and cut into strips
2 whole roasted red peppers, drained, patted dry and cut into strips
1 cup (4 ounces) shredded Monterey Jack cheese
1 teaspoon ground cumin
1 teaspoon ground coriander
½ teaspoon dry mustard
¼ teaspoon salt
¼ teaspoon black pepper
4 eggs
1 cup sour cream
Salsa Colorado (recipe follows)

*Corn meal may be substituted for masa harina de maiz. Look for masa harina in the Mexican section of the grocery store.

Combine flour, masa harina de maiz and salt in food processor fitted with knife blade; cover and process until blended. Sprinkle butter evenly over flour mixture; cover and process until mixture resembles coarse meal. Pour ice water evenly over mixture; cover and pulse until dough holds together. Form dough into a ball; press evenly on bottom and halfway up sides of 10×3-inch springform pan. Bake at 400°F for 15 minutes. Let cool.

Sauté onions in oil until lightly browned and tender. Arrange chiles and red peppers on bottom of crust. Sprinkle with cheese. Combine spices, salt and black pepper; sprinkle half of spices evenly over cheese. Arrange onions on top; sprinkle with remaining spices. Beat eggs and sour cream; pour evenly over onions. Bake at 325°F for 45 to 50 minutes or until set. Let cool 15 minutes before cutting. Serve with Salsa Colorado.

Makes 8 to 10 servings

Salsa Colorado

1 (16-ounce) can tomato purée
½ cup water
½ (7-ounce) can chipotle peppers in adobo sauce
2 medium onions, chopped
4 cloves garlic, crushed
¼ teaspoon salt

Combine all ingredients in medium saucepan; bring to a boil. Cover; reduce heat and simmer 20 minutes. Purée in blender or food processor bowl. Serve with Tamale Pie.

Makes 8 to 10 servings

Favorite recipe from **National Onion Association**

Veggie Tostadas

1 tablespoon olive oil
1 cup chopped onion
1 cup chopped celery
2 large cloves garlic, chopped
1 can (15½ ounces) red kidney beans, drained
1 can (15½ ounces) Great Northern beans, drained
1 can (14½ ounces) salsa-style diced tomatoes
2 teaspoons mild chili powder
1 teaspoon cumin
2 tablespoons chopped fresh cilantro
6 small corn tortillas
   Toppings: shredded lettuce, chopped tomatoes, shredded Cheddar cheese and sour cream

Heat oil in large skillet over medium heat. Add onion, celery and garlic. Cook and stir 8 minutes or until softened. Add beans and tomatoes. Stir to blend. Add chili powder and cumin; stir. Reduce heat to medium-low. Simmer 30 minutes, stirring occasionally until thickened.

Preheat oven to 400°F.

While bean mixture simmers, place tortillas in single layer directly on oven rack. Bake 10 to 12 minutes or until crisp. Place one tortilla on each plate. Spoon bean mixture evenly over each one. Top with lettuce, tomatoes, Cheddar cheese and sour cream to taste. *Makes 6 servings*

Mexican Tortilla Stack-Ups

1 tablespoon vegetable oil
½ cup chopped onion
1 can (15 ounces) black beans, drained and rinsed
1 can (14½ ounces) Mexican- or Italian-style diced tomatoes, undrained
1 cup frozen corn
1 envelope (1¼ ounces) taco seasoning mix
6 corn tortillas (6 inches)
2 cups (8 ounces) shredded Cheddar cheese with taco seasonings
1 cup water
  Sour cream (optional)
  Sliced black olives (optional)

Preheat oven to 350°F. Spray 13×9-inch baking dish with nonstick cooking spray.

Heat oil in large skillet over medium-high heat until hot. Add onion; cook and stir 3 minutes or until tender. Add beans, tomatoes with juice, corn and taco seasoning mix. Bring to a boil over high heat. Reduce heat to low and simmer 5 minutes.

Place 2 tortillas side by side in prepared dish. Top each tortilla with about ½ cup bean mixture. Sprinkle evenly with ⅓ of cheese. Repeat layers twice, creating 2 tortilla stacks each 3 tortillas high.

Pour water along sides of tortillas.

Cover tightly with foil and bake 30 to 35 minutes or until heated through. Cut into wedges to serve. Serve with sour cream and black olives, if desired. *Makes 6 servings*

Mexican Tortilla Stack-Ups

Bell Pepper Nachos

1 medium green bell pepper
1 medium yellow or red bell pepper
  Nonstick cooking spray
2 Italian plum tomatoes, seeded and chopped
⅓ cup finely chopped onion
1 teaspoon chili powder
½ teaspoon ground cumin
1½ cups cooked white rice
½ cup (2 ounces) shredded reduced-fat Monterey Jack cheese
¼ cup chopped fresh cilantro
2 teaspoons jalapeño pepper sauce *or* ¼ teaspoon hot pepper sauce
½ cup (2 ounces) shredded reduced-fat sharp Cheddar cheese

1. Spray large nonstick baking sheets with cooking spray; set aside.

2. Cut bell peppers into 2×1½-inch strips; cut strips into bite-sized triangles (each bell pepper strip should yield 2 or 3 triangles).

3. Spray large nonstick skillet with nonstick cooking spray. Add tomatoes, onion, chili powder and cumin. Cook over medium heat 3 minutes or until onion is tender, stirring occasionally. Remove from heat. Stir in rice, Monterey Jack cheese, cilantro and pepper sauce.

4. Top each pepper triangle with approximately 2 tablespoons rice mixture; sprinkle with Cheddar cheese. Place on prepared baking sheets; cover with plastic wrap. Refrigerate up to 8 hours before serving.

5. When ready to serve, preheat broiler. Remove plastic wrap. Broil nachos, 6 to 8 inches from heat, 3 to 4 minutes (or bake at 400°F 8 to 10 minutes) or until cheese is bubbly and rice is heated through. Transfer to serving plate; garnish, if desired.   *Makes 8 servings*

Bell Pepper Nachos

Spicy Vegetable Quesadillas

1 small zucchini, chopped
½ cup chopped green bell pepper
½ cup chopped onion
2 cloves garlic, minced
½ teaspoon chili powder
½ teaspoon ground cumin
8 (6-inch) flour tortillas
1 cup (4 ounces) shredded reduced-fat Cheddar cheese
¼ cup chopped fresh cilantro

1. Spray large nonstick skillet with cooking spray. Heat over medium heat until hot. Add zucchini, pepper, onion, garlic, chili powder and cumin; cook and stir 3 to 4 minutes or until vegetables are crisp-tender. Remove vegetables and set aside; wipe skillet clean.

2. Spoon vegetable mixture evenly over half of each tortilla. Sprinkle each evenly with cheese and cilantro. Fold each tortilla in half.

3. Spray same skillet with cooking spray. Add tortillas and heat 1 to 2 minutes per side over medium heat or until lightly browned. Cut into thirds before serving.   *Makes 8 servings*

Spicy Vegetable Quesadillas

Cornmeal Squares with Salsa

1 cup yellow cornmeal
1 teaspoon chili powder
4 cups water
1 teaspoon salt
1 cup (4 ounces) grated Monterey Jack cheese
1 (4-ounce) can green chilies, drained, chopped and patted dry
¼ cup chopped fresh cilantro
6 tablespoons vegetable oil, divided
1 (11-ounce) jar NEWMAN'S OWN® All Natural Salsa

In small bowl, combine cornmeal and chili powder; set aside. In large saucepan, heat water and salt over medium heat to boiling. Sprinkle cornmeal mixture ¼ cup at a time into water, whisking constantly. Cook, stirring constantly with wooden spoon, until thickened, about 10 minutes. Stir in cheese, chilies and cilantro. Spread evenly in oiled 15×10×½-inch baking pan. Refrigerate to cool completely. Cut cooked cornmeal into fifteen 3×3¼-inch squares.

In large, nonstick saucepan, heat 2 tablespoons oil over medium-high heat. Add five squares and cook, turning once, until golden brown, 8 to 10 minutes. Repeat with remaining oil and squares. Serve with Newman's Own® All Natural Salsa.

Makes 4 to 6 servings

Fiesta Broccoli, Rice and Beans

    2 cups frozen broccoli florets
    2 cups uncooked instant rice
    ½ teaspoon chili powder
    1 cup salsa or picante sauce
    1 can (19 ounces) black beans, rinsed and drained
    ¼ cup (1 ounce) shredded Cheddar or pepper-Jack cheese

1. Place broccoli and 2 tablespoons water in microwavable dish. Cover loosely with plastic wrap; cook at HIGH 4 to 5 minutes or until crisp-tender.

2. Cook rice according to package directions, adding chili powder to cooking water.

3. Stir salsa and black beans into hot cooked rice. Top each serving of rice and beans with broccoli and cheese.
Makes 4 servings

Prep and Cook Time: 20 minutes

Calabacitas

    2 tablespoons vegetable oil
    2 medium yellow crookneck squash, cut into ¼-inch slices
    2 medium zucchini, cut into ¼-inch slices
    1 medium onion, coarsely chopped
    1 clove garlic, minced
    1 can (8 ounces) whole kernel corn, drained
    ¼ cup diced green chilies
    ½ teaspoon salt
    ¼ teaspoon dried oregano
    ⅛ teaspoon black pepper
    ½ cup (2 ounces) shredded mild Cheddar cheese

Heat oil in large skillet over medium heat. Add squash, zucchini, onion and garlic. Cook, stirring occasionally, until onion is tender. Reduce heat. Cover; continue cooking 10 minutes or until squash are barely tender. Add corn, chilies, salt, oregano and pepper. Cook 3 minutes or until hot. Sprinkle with cheese; heat just until cheese melts.
Makes 4 to 6 servings

Vegetable Empanadas with Salsa

2 tablespoons olive oil
1 cup frozen diced hash brown potatoes
1 red bell pepper, chopped
1 green bell pepper, chopped
1 onion, chopped
1 package (8 ounces) sliced mushrooms
2 teaspoons bottled minced garlic
1½ teaspoons ground cumin
½ teaspoon salt
½ teaspoon ground nutmeg
½ teaspoon black pepper
¼ teaspoon ground red pepper
1 package (17 ounces) frozen puff pastry sheets, thawed
½ cup (2 ounces) shredded Monterey Jack cheese
3 tablespoons milk
1 cup salsa

1. Heat oil in large nonstick skillet over medium heat. Add potatoes, bell peppers, onion, mushrooms, garlic and spices; cook and stir 5 minutes. Let cool to room temperature.

2. Preheat oven to 400°F. Unfold pastry sheets on floured surface. Roll each sheet into 12-inch square with lightly floured rolling pin; cut each square into 4 squares with sharp knife. Place about ¼ cup filling in corner of each square; sprinkle with 1 tablespoon cheese.

3. Brush small amount of milk on edges of pastry squares. Fold opposite corners over filling to meet each other, forming triangles. Press edges with fork to seal. Cut small slit in top of each triangle with knife. (At this point, empanadas may be covered and refrigerated up to 24 hours or frozen up to 1 month.)

4. Place triangles on *ungreased* baking sheets; brush tops with remaining milk. Bake 15 to 20 minutes or until puffed and golden. Serve with salsa. *Makes 8 servings*

Vegetable Empanadas with Salsa

Chili Relleno Casserole

1½ cups (6 ounces) SARGENTO® Light 4 Cheese Mexican Shredded Cheese or SARGENTO®
    Light Shredded Cheese for Tacos, divided
1 can (12 ounces) evaporated skim milk
¾ cup (6 ounces) fat-free liquid egg substitute *or* 3 eggs, beaten
6 (7-inch) corn tortillas, torn into 2-inch pieces
2 cans (4 ounces each) chopped green chilies
½ cup mild chunky salsa
¼ teaspoon salt (optional)
2 tablespoons chopped fresh cilantro
    Light or fat-free sour cream (optional)

1. Coat 10-inch deep dish pie plate or 8-inch square baking dish with nonstick cooking spray. In medium bowl, combine 1 cup cheese, milk, egg substitute, tortillas, chilies, salsa and salt, if desired. Mix well; pour into prepared dish.

2. Bake at 375°F 30 to 32 minutes or until set. Remove from oven; sprinkle with remaining ½ cup cheese and cilantro. Return to oven; bake 1 minute or until cheese is melted. Serve with sour cream, if desired.

Makes 4 servings

Chili Relleno Casserole

Spinach and Mushroom Enchiladas

 2 packages (10 ounces each) frozen chopped spinach, thawed
1½ cups sliced mushrooms
 1 can (15 ounces) pinto beans, drained and rinsed
 3 teaspoons chili powder, divided
 ¼ teaspoon red pepper flakes
 1 can (8 ounces) reduced-sodium tomato sauce
 2 tablespoons water
 ½ teaspoon hot pepper sauce
 8 (8-inch) corn tortillas
 1 cup shredded Monterey Jack cheese
   Shredded lettuce (optional)
   Chopped tomatoes (optional)
   Reduced-fat sour cream (optional)

1. Combine spinach, mushrooms, beans, 2 teaspoons chili powder and red pepper flakes in large skillet over medium heat. Cook and stir 5 minutes; remove from heat.

2. Combine tomato sauce, water, remaining 1 teaspoon chili powder and pepper sauce in medium skillet. Dip tortillas into tomato sauce mixture; stack tortillas on waxed paper.

3. Divide spinach filling into 8 portions. Spoon onto center of tortillas; roll up and place in 11×8-inch microwavable dish. (Secure rolls with wooden toothpicks, if desired.) Spread remaining tomato sauce mixture over enchiladas.

4. Cover with vented plastic wrap. Microwave at MEDIUM (50%) 10 minutes or until heated through. Sprinkle with cheese. Microwave, uncovered, at MEDIUM 3 minutes or until cheese is melted. Serve with lettuce, tomatoes and sour cream. *Makes 4 servings*

Spinach and Mushroom Enchiladas

Arriba Stuffed Bell Peppers

4 medium green bell peppers
1 tablespoon butter or margarine
½ cup chopped onion
½ cup chopped green bell pepper
1 cup long-grain rice
1½ cups water
1 can (8 ounces) tomato sauce
1 teaspoon LAWRY'S® Seasoned Salt
1 teaspoon LAWRY'S® Seasoned Pepper
1 can (2¼ ounces) sliced black olives, drained
½ cup sliced green onions

Cut tops off bell peppers and hollow out. In large saucepan, parboil peppers in boiling water to cover 1 minute; set aside. In medium saucepan, heat butter. Add onion and chopped bell pepper and cook over medium-high heat until tender-crisp. Add rice, water, tomato sauce, Seasoned Salt and Seasoned Pepper. Bring to a boil over medium-high heat; reduce heat to low and simmer, covered, 20 minutes, or until all moisture is absorbed and rice is tender. Stir in olives and green onions. Spoon into hollowed-out bell pepper shells. Place in baking dish, cover with foil and bake in 350°F oven 15 to 20 minutes or until heated through.   *Makes 4 servings*

Serving Suggestion: Garnish with parsley sprigs.

Cheese Enchiladas with Green Chiles

1¼ cups (10-ounce can) ORTEGA® Enchilada Sauce

1 cup ORTEGA® Salsa Prima-Garden Style Mild

15 (6-inch) corn tortillas

1 pound Monterey Jack cheese, sliced into 15 strips

1 can (7 ounces) ORTEGA® Whole Green Chiles, sliced into 3 strips

1 cup (4 ounces) shredded Monterey Jack cheese

PREHEAT oven to 350°F.

COMBINE enchilada sauce and salsa in medium bowl; mix well. Pour *1½ cups* sauce mixture onto bottom of ungreased 13×9-inch baking pan.

HEAT tortillas, one at a time, in lightly greased medium skillet over medium-high heat for 20 seconds on each side or until soft. Place 1 strip cheese and 1 strip chile in center of each tortilla; roll up. Place seam-side down in baking pan. Repeat with remaining tortillas, cheese and chiles. Ladle *remaining* sauce mixture over enchiladas; sprinkle with shredded cheese.

BAKE, covered, for 20 minutes. Remove cover; bake for additional 5 minutes or until heated through and cheese is melted.

Makes 6 to 8 servings

Chile Cheese Puff

¾ cup all-purpose flour
1½ teaspoons baking powder
9 eggs
1 pound (16 ounces) shredded Monterey Jack cheese
2 cups (1 pint) 1% milkfat cottage cheese
2 cans (4 ounces each) diced green chilies, drained
1½ teaspoons sugar
¼ teaspoon salt
⅛ teaspoon hot pepper sauce
1 cup salsa

Preheat oven to 350°F. Spray 13×9-inch baking dish with nonstick cooking spray.

Combine flour and baking powder in small bowl.

Whisk eggs in large bowl until blended; add Monterey Jack, cottage cheese, chilies, sugar, salt and hot pepper sauce. Add flour mixture; stir just until combined. Pour into prepared dish.

Bake, uncovered, 45 minutes or until egg mixture is set. Let stand 5 minutes before serving. Serve with salsa.

Makes 8 servings

Santa Fe Rice

2½ cups hot cooked MINUTE® Original Rice
1 cup canned black *or* red beans
1 cup TACO BELL® HOME ORIGINALS®* Thick 'N Chunky Salsa

*TACO BELL and HOME ORIGINALS are registered trademarks owned and licensed by Taco Bell Corp.

MIX all ingredients. Serve immediately.

Makes 4 servings

Prep Time: 10 minutes

Chile Cheese Puff

Veggie Kabobs with Tex-Mex Polenta

Polenta

2¾ cups water
¾ cup yellow cornmeal
½ teaspoon salt
1 can (4 ounces) chopped green chilies, drained
½ cup (2 ounces) shredded Monterey Jack cheese
2 tablespoons shredded Cheddar cheese
2 tablespoons grated Parmesan cheese

Veggie Kabobs

½ cup olive oil
¼ cup cider vinegar
1 teaspoon salt
¾ teaspoon garlic powder
½ teaspoon black pepper
3 large bell peppers, cut into 1½-inch pieces
1 medium red onion, cut into 1-inch wedges
8 ounces fresh mushrooms

1. Combine water, cornmeal and salt in large microwavable bowl. Cover tightly; microwave at HIGH 10 to 12 minutes, stirring halfway through cooking time. Stir in chilies and Monterey Jack cheese. Cover; let stand 2 minutes. Grease 9-inch casserole. Spread cornmeal mixture into prepared casserole. Cover; refrigerate 2 hours or until firm.

2. Preheat broiler. Turn polenta out of casserole; cut into 6 wedges. Grease small baking sheet. Place polenta on baking sheet. Broil 6 inches from heat 5 to 6 minutes per side. Sprinkle with Cheddar and Parmesan cheeses.

3. Soak 8 to 10 wooden skewers in water. Combine oil, vinegar, salt, garlic powder and black pepper in medium bowl. Alternately thread bell peppers, onion and mushrooms onto skewers. Arrange skewers in shallow pan. Pour oil marinade over skewers. Cover; refrigerate at least 2 hours or overnight.

4. To complete recipe, preheat broiler. Transfer skewers to large baking sheet. Broil 8 to 10 minutes or until vegetables begin to brown. Serve with polenta. *Makes 4 to 6 servings*

Make-Ahead Time: 2 hours to 1 day before serving
Final Prep and Cook Time: 30 minutes

Veggie Kabobs with Tex-Mex Polenta

Light Entrées

Chipotle Chili con Carne

¾ pound lean cubed beef stew meat
1 tablespoon chili powder
1 tablespoon ground cumin
  Nonstick cooking spray
1 can (about 14 ounces) reduced-sodium beef broth
1 tablespoon minced canned chipotle chilies in adobo sauce, or to taste
1 can (14½ ounces) diced tomatoes, undrained
1 large green bell pepper *or* 2 poblano chili peppers, cut into pieces
2 cans (16 ounces each) pinto or red beans, rinsed and drained
  Chopped fresh cilantro (optional)

1. Toss beef in combined chili powder and cumin. Coat large saucepan with cooking spray; heat over medium heat. Add beef; cook 5 minutes, stirring occasionally. Add beef broth and chipotle chilies with sauce; bring to a boil. Reduce heat; cover and simmer 1 hour 15 minutes or until beef is very tender.

2. With slotted spoon, transfer beef to carving board, leaving juices in saucepan. Using two forks, shred beef. Return beef to saucepan; add tomatoes and bell pepper. Bring to a boil; stir in beans. Simmer, uncovered, 20 minutes or until bell pepper is tender. Garnish with cilantro, if desired.

Makes 6 servings

Chipotle Chili con Carne

Stacked Burrito Pie

½ cup GUILTLESS GOURMET® Mild Black Bean Dip
2 teaspoons water
5 low-fat flour tortillas (6 inches each)
½ cup nonfat sour cream or plain yogurt
½ cup GUILTLESS GOURMET® Roasted Red Pepper Salsa
1¼ cups (5 ounces) shredded low-fat Monterey Jack cheese
4 cups shredded iceberg or romaine lettuce
½ cup GUILTLESS GOURMET® Salsa (Roasted Red Pepper or Southwestern Grill)
Lime slices and chili pepper (optional)

Preheat oven to 350°F. Combine bean dip and 2 teaspoons water in small bowl; mix well. Line 7½-inch springform pan with 1 tortilla. Spread 2 tablespoons bean dip mixture over tortilla, then spread with 2 tablespoons sour cream and 2 tablespoons red pepper salsa. Sprinkle with ¼ cup cheese. Repeat layers 3 more times. Place remaining tortilla on top and sprinkle with remaining ¼ cup cheese.

Bake 40 minutes or until heated through. (Place sheet of foil under springform pan to catch any juices that may seep through the bottom.) Cool slightly before unmolding. To serve, cut into 4 quarters. Place 1 cup lettuce on 4 serving plates. Top each serving with 1 quarter burrito pie and 2 tablespoons salsa. Garnish with lime slices and pepper, if desired. *Makes 4 servings*

Rio Grande Bean Enchiladas

3 teaspoons olive oil, divided
2 cups chopped onions, divided
1 can (14½ ounces) crushed tomatoes
1 can (6 ounces) tomato paste
2 tablespoons chili powder
1 tablespoon prepared green salsa
2 teaspoons ground cumin, divided
1 teaspoon sugar
⅛ teaspoon black pepper
2 cloves garlic, finely chopped
1 can (about 15 ounces) black beans, rinsed, drained and mashed
1 cup plain nonfat yogurt
8 (6-inch) corn tortillas

1. Heat 2 teaspoons oil in large saucepan over medium-high heat until hot. Add 1 cup onions. Cook and stir 5 minutes or until tender. Stir in tomatoes, tomato paste, chili powder, salsa, 1 teaspoon cumin, sugar and pepper. Reduce heat to medium-low. Simmer 30 minutes.

2. Heat remaining 1 teaspoon oil in large skillet over medium-high heat until hot. Add remaining 1 cup onions, 1 teaspoon cumin and garlic. Cook and stir 5 minutes or until onions are tender. Stir in beans. Cook 5 minutes or until heated through, stirring occasionally. Remove skillet from heat. Stir in yogurt.

3. Preheat oven to 375°F. Spoon bean mixture evenly down centers of tortillas. Roll up tortillas; place in medium baking dish. Top with sauce.

4. Bake 20 minutes. Serve with dollops of nonfat sour cream and cilantro, if desired. Garnish with cilantro and red pepper strips, if desired.   *Makes 4 servings*

Rio Grande Bean Enchiladas

Tamale Pie

Biscuit Topping
- ½ cup white or yellow cornmeal
- ½ cup buttermilk
- ⅓ cup all-purpose flour
- 1 egg white, slightly beaten
- 1 tablespoon sugar
- ½ jalapeño pepper,* seeded and chopped
- 1 teaspoon baking powder

Filling
- Nonstick cooking spray
- 1 green bell pepper, chopped
- ¾ cup chopped green onions
- 2 cloves garlic, finely chopped
- 1½ cups canned crushed tomatoes
- 1 can (about 15 ounces) pinto beans, rinsed and drained
- ¼ pound cooked ground turkey breast
- 2 teaspoons chili powder
- 1 teaspoon ground cumin
- ¼ teaspoon black pepper

*Jalapeño peppers can sting and irritate the skin. Wear rubber gloves when handling peppers and do not touch eyes. Wash hands after handling.

1. Preheat oven to 425°F. Spray 9-inch pie plate with nonstick cooking spray; set aside.

2. For topping, combine all topping ingredients in large bowl until well blended; set aside.

3. For filling, spray large nonstick skillet with cooking spray. Heat over medium heat until hot. Add bell pepper, onions and garlic. Cook and stir 5 minutes or until vegetables are tender. Add tomatoes, beans, turkey, chili powder, cumin and black pepper. Cook and stir 5 minutes or until heated through.

4. Spoon vegetable mixture into prepared pie plate. Drop heaping tablespoonfuls topping around outer edge of filling; flatten with back of spoon to form biscuits.

5. Bake 25 minutes or until biscuits are golden brown. Let stand 5 minutes before serving.

Makes 4 servings

Lime-Grilled Chicken with Chive Polenta

1 tablespoon chopped fresh parsley
1 tablespoon olive oil
1 teaspoon minced garlic
1 teaspoon grated lime peel
3 cups fat-free reduced-sodium chicken broth
¾ cup yellow cornmeal
¼ cup low-fat sour cream
2 tablespoons snipped fresh chives
4 boneless skinless chicken breast halves
½ teaspoon salt
1 cup prepared salsa

1. Combine parsley, olive oil, garlic and lime peel in small bowl; mix well; set aside.

2. Bring chicken broth to a boil in large saucepan. Gradually stir in cornmeal. Reduce heat to low; cook, stirring frequently, 15 minutes or until mixture is thick and pulls away from side of pan. (Mixture may be lumpy.) Stir in sour cream and chives; cover, set aside and keep warm.

3. Sprinkle chicken with salt. To prevent sticking, spray grid with nonstick cooking spray. Prepare grill for direct grilling. Place chicken on grid, 3 to 4 inches from medium-hot coals. Grill 5 to 7 minutes on each side or until no longer pink in center. Spread parsley mixture evenly over both sides of chicken; cook 1 minute longer on each side.

4. Serve chicken with polenta; top with salsa.

Makes 4 servings

White Chili Pilaf

½ pound lean ground beef
  Nonstick cooking spray
½ pound bulk turkey sausage
1 cup finely chopped green bell pepper
2 to 3 tablespoons seeded, minced jalapeño peppers*
2 teaspoons minced garlic
2 teaspoons ground cumin
½ teaspoon dried oregano leaves
2¼ cups water
2 teaspoons chicken flavor bouillon granules
1 cup uncooked white basmati rice
1 cup rinsed and drained canned Great Northern beans
1 cup sliced green onions
½ cup minced fresh cilantro
6 tablespoons nonfat sour cream
¾ cup diced seeded tomato
½ cup plus 1 tablespoon shredded reduced-fat Colby-Jack cheese

*Jalapeño peppers can sting and irritate the skin. Wear rubber gloves when handling peppers and do not touch eyes. Wash hands after handling.

1. Spray large nonstick skillet with cooking spray; heat over medium heat until hot. Add beef and sausage; cook 5 minutes or until meat is no longer pink, stirring to crumble. Remove meat from skillet.

2. Spray large saucepan with cooking spray; add peppers and garlic. Cook and stir over medium heat 5 minutes or until peppers are tender. Stir in cumin and oregano; cook and stir 1 minute. Stir in water and bouillon granules; bring to a boil over high heat. Stir in rice. Cover; reduce heat to medium-low. Simmer 15 minutes.

3. Add meat, beans and onions to saucepan; cover. Simmer 5 minutes or until rice is tender. Remove saucepan from heat; stir in cilantro. Cover; let stand 5 minutes. Top each serving evenly with sour cream, tomato and cheese before serving. *Makes 6 servings*

White Chili Pilaf

Chili Beef & Red Pepper Fajitas with Chipotle Salsa

6 ounces top sirloin steak, thinly sliced
½ lime
1½ teaspoons chili powder
½ teaspoon ground cumin
½ cup diced plum tomatoes
¼ cup mild picante sauce
½ canned chipotle chili pepper in adobo sauce
   Nonstick cooking spray
½ cup sliced onion
½ red bell pepper, cut in thin strips
2 (10-inch) fat-free flour tortillas, warmed
¼ cup nonfat sour cream
2 tablespoons chopped cilantro leaves (optional)

1. Place steak on plate. Squeeze lime over steak; sprinkle with chili powder and cumin. Toss to coat well; let stand 10 minutes.

2. Meanwhile, to prepare salsa, combine tomatoes and picante sauce in small bowl. Place chipotle on small plate. Using fork, mash completely. Stir mashed chipotle into tomato mixture.

3. Coat 12-inch skillet with cooking spray. Heat over high heat until hot. Add onion and pepper; cook and stir 3 minutes or until beginning to blacken on edges; remove from skillet. Lightly spray skillet with cooking spray. Add beef; cook and stir 1 minute. Return onion and pepper to skillet; cook 1 minute longer.

4. Place ½ of the beef mixture in center of each tortilla; top with ¼ cup salsa, 2 tablespoons sour cream and cilantro, if desired. Fold or serve open-faced. *Makes 2 servings*

Note: For a less spicy salsa, use less chipotle chili or eliminate it completely.

Chili Beef & Red Pepper Fajita with Chipotle Salsa

Easy Tex-Mex Bake

8 ounces uncooked thin mostaccioli
Nonstick cooking spray
1 pound ground turkey breast
⅔ cup bottled medium or mild salsa
1 package (10 ounces) frozen corn, thawed and drained
1 container (16 ounces) low-fat cottage cheese
1 egg
1 tablespoon minced fresh cilantro
½ teaspoon white pepper
¼ teaspoon ground cumin

1. Cook pasta according to package directions, omitting salt. Drain and rinse well; set aside.

2. Spray large nonstick skillet with cooking spray. Add turkey; cook until no longer pink, about 5 minutes. Stir in salsa and corn. Remove from heat.

3. Preheat oven to 350°F. Combine cottage cheese, egg, cilantro, white pepper and cumin in small bowl.

4. Spoon ½ turkey mixture in bottom of 11×7-inch baking dish. Top with pasta. Spoon cottage cheese mixture over pasta. Top with remaining turkey mixture. Sprinkle Monterey Jack cheese over casserole.

5. Bake 25 to 30 minutes or until heated through.   *Makes 6 servings*

Easy Tex-Mex Bake

Black Bean and Tempeh Burritos with Sauce

2 teaspoons olive oil
½ cup chopped onion
½ cup chopped green bell pepper
2 cloves garlic, minced
2 teaspoons chili powder
1 teaspoon dried oregano leaves
½ teaspoon dried coriander leaves
2 cans (14½ ounces each) no-salt-added stewed tomatoes
1 can (15 ounces) black beans, rinsed and drained
¼ pound tempeh, diced
¼ cup minced onion
¼ teaspoon black pepper
½ teaspoon ground cumin
8 flour tortillas (6-inch diameter)

For sauce, heat oil in large nonstick skillet over medium heat. Add chopped onion, bell pepper and garlic; cook and stir 5 minutes or until onion is tender. Add chili powder; cook 1 minute. Add oregano, coriander and tomatoes; cook and stir over medium heat 15 minutes.

Preheat oven to 350°F. Place beans in medium bowl; mash well with fork. Mix in tempeh, minced onion, black pepper and cumin. Add about ¼ cup sauce to hold mixture together.

Soften tortillas if necessary.* Spread ⅓ cup bean mixture down center of each tortilla. Roll up tortillas; place in single layer in shallow baking dish. Pour remaining sauce over burritos. Bake 15 minutes or until heated through.   *Makes 4 servings*

*To soften tortillas, wrap stack of tortillas in foil. Heat in preheated 350°F oven about 10 minutes or until softened.

 Señor Says: **Tempeh is a fermented soybean cake with a yeasty, nutty flavor and a texture similar to that of soft tofu. It is available at health food stores.**

Pollo Verde Casserole

2 boneless skinless chicken breast halves (about 4 ounces each)
1 teaspoon canola oil
1 medium onion, chopped
½ medium bell pepper, chopped
1 teaspoon chopped garlic
1 cup GUILTLESS GOURMET® Salsa (Roasted Red Pepper or Southwestern Grill), divided
½ cup low-fat sour cream, divided
   Nonstick cooking spray
1 cup (3.5 ounces) crushed GUILTLESS GOURMET® Unsalted Baked Tortilla Chips, divided

Cut chicken into 1-inch cubes. Heat oil in large skillet over medium-high heat until hot. Add chicken cubes, onion, pepper and garlic; cook and stir about 5 to 10 minutes or until chicken turns white and onion is translucent. Remove from heat.

Combine ½ cup salsa and ¼ cup sour cream in small bowl until blended. Stir salsa mixture into chicken mixture.

Preheat oven to 325°F. Coat 2-quart glass casserole dish with cooking spray. Sprinkle ½ cup crushed chips into prepared casserole dish. Spread chicken mixture over crushed chips. Top with remaining crushed chips, then with remaining ½ cup salsa.

Bake 30 minutes or cover with plastic wrap and microwave on HIGH (100% power) 12 minutes or until heated through. Let stand 5 minutes before serving. To serve, divide mixture among 4 serving plates. Top each serving with a dollop of remaining ¼ cup sour cream. *Makes 4 servings*

Black Bean Tostadas

1 cup rinsed, drained canned black beans, mashed
2 teaspoons chili powder
  Nonstick cooking spray
4 (8-inch) corn tortillas
1 cup washed, torn romaine lettuce leaves
1 cup chopped seeded tomato
½ cup chopped onion
½ cup plain nonfat yogurt
2 jalapeño peppers,* seeded, finely chopped

*Jalapeño peppers can sting and irritate the skin. Wear rubber gloves when handling peppers and do not touch eyes. Wash hands after handling.

1. Combine beans and chili powder in small saucepan. Cook 5 minutes over medium heat or until heated through, stirring occasionally.

2. Spray large nonstick skillet with cooking spray. Heat over medium heat until hot. Sprinkle tortillas with water; place in skillet, one at a time. Cook 20 to 30 seconds or until hot and pliable, turning once.

3. Spread bean mixture evenly over tortillas; layer with lettuce, tomato, onion, yogurt and peppers. Garnish with cilantro, sliced tomatoes and peppers, if desired. Serve immediately.

Makes 4 servings

Black Bean Tostada

Fajitas

Fajita Marinade (recipe page 282)
1 pound flank steak
Salsa Cruda (recipe page 174)
6 (10-inch) flour tortillas *or* **12 (7-inch) flour tortillas**
4 bell peppers, any color, halved
1 large bunch green onions
1 cup coarsely chopped fresh cilantro
1 ripe avocado, thinly sliced (optional)
6 tablespoons low-fat sour cream (optional)

1. Combine Fajita Marinade and flank steak in resealable plastic food storage bag. Press air from bag and seal. Refrigerate 30 minutes or up to 24 hours.

2. Prepare Salsa Cruda; set aside. Wrap tortillas in foil in stacks of 3; set aside.

3. Drain marinade from meat into small saucepan. Bring to a boil over high heat. Remove from heat.

4. Spray cold grid of grill with nonstick cooking spray. Adjust grid 4 to 6 inches above heat. Preheat grill to medium-high heat. Place meat in center of grid. Place bell peppers, skin side down, around meat; cover. Grill bell peppers 6 minutes or until skin is spotted brown. Turn over and continue grilling 6 to 8 minutes or until tender. Move to sides of grill to keep warm while meat finishes grilling.

5. Continue to grill meat, basting frequently with marinade, 8 minutes or until browned on bottom. Turn over; grill 8 to 10 minutes or until slightly pink in center.

6. During the last 4 minutes of grilling, brush green onions with remaining marinade and place on grid; grill 1 to 2 minutes or until browned in spots. Turn over; grill 1 to 2 minutes or until tender.

7. Place packets of tortillas on grid; heat about 5 minutes. Slice bell peppers and onions into thin 2-inch-long pieces. Thinly slice meat across the grain.

8. Place each tortilla on plate. Place meat, bell peppers, onions, Salsa Cruda and cilantro in center of each tortilla. Fold bottom 3 inches of each tortilla up over filling; fold sides completely over filling to enclose. Serve with avocado and sour cream, if desired. *Makes 6 servings*

continued on page 282

Fajitas

Fajitas, continued

Fajita Marinade

½ cup lime juice *or* ¼ cup lime juice and ¼ cup tequilla or beer
1 tablespoon dried oregano leaves
1 tablespoon minced garlic
2 teaspoons ground cumin
2 teaspoons black pepper

Combine lime juice, oregano, garlic, cumin and black pepper in 1-cup glass measure.

Makes 1 cup

Mexican Barbecued Lamb Steaks

1 teaspoon vegetable oil
½ cup finely chopped red bell pepper
¼ cup finely chopped onion
¼ cup packed brown sugar
1 can (15 ounces) tomato sauce
1 can (4 ounces) diced green chilies
1 teaspoon Worcestershire sauce
½ teaspoon chili powder
¼ teaspoon garlic powder
¼ teaspoon black pepper
¼ teaspoon hot pepper sauce
3 American lamb sirloin steaks *or* 6 shoulder chops (2 pounds), cut ¾ to 1 inch thick

Heat oil over medium-high heat in large nonstick skillet. Add bell pepper and onion; cook and stir until onion is transparent. Add brown sugar; stir until melted. Add tomato sauce, green chilies, Worcestershire sauce, chili powder, garlic powder, black pepper and hot pepper sauce; heat thoroughly. Brush on steaks or chops. Grill over moderate coals, 8 to 10 minutes, basting chops frequently with sauce.

Makes 6 servings

Favorite recipe from **American Lamb Council**

Citrus Chicken and Bell Pepper Fajitas

1 teaspoon CRISCO® Oil*
4 boneless, skinless chicken breast halves, cut into strips (about 1 pound)
2 medium green bell peppers, cut into strips
1 large onion, cut into 1-inch pieces
2 cloves garlic, minced
½ cup fresh lime juice
1 teaspoon ground cumin
1 teaspoon dried oregano leaves
⅛ teaspoon black pepper
8 (7- to 8-inch) flour tortillas
   Salt (optional)
½ cup salsa
¼ cup chopped green onions with tops

*Use your favorite Crisco Oil product.

1. Heat oil in large skillet on medium-high heat. Add chicken, green peppers, onion and garlic. Cook and stir 2 minutes.

2. Reduce heat to low. Add lime juice, cumin, oregano and black pepper. Simmer 7 minutes or until chicken is no longer pink in center.

3. Warm tortillas, 15 seconds per side, in nonstick skillet on medium heat. Place on serving plate. Use slotted spoon to transfer chicken mixture to tortillas. Season with salt, if desired. Top with salsa and green onions. Fold up bottom, then fold in sides to enclose.   *Makes 4 servings*

Black Beans & Rice-Stuffed Chilies

Nonstick olive oil cooking spray
2 large poblano chili peppers*
½ can (15½ ounces) black beans, drained and rinsed
½ cup cooked brown rice
⅓ cup mild or medium chunky salsa
⅓ cup shredded pepper Jack cheese or reduced-fat Cheddar cheese, divided

*Poblano peppers can sting and irritate the skin. Wear rubber gloves when handling peppers and do not touch eyes. Wash hands after handling.

1. Preheat oven to 375°F. Lightly spray shallow baking pan with cooking spray.

2. Cut thin slice from one side of each pepper; chop pepper slices. In medium saucepan cook peppers in boiling water 6 minutes. Drain and rinse with cold water. Remove and discard seeds and membranes.

3. Stir together beans, rice, salsa, chopped pepper and ¼ cup cheese. Spoon into peppers, mounding mixture. Place peppers in prepared pan. Cover with foil. Bake 12 to 15 minutes or until heated through.

4. Sprinkle with remaining cheese. Bake 2 minutes more or until cheese melts.   *Makes 2 servings*

Black Beans & Rice-Stuffed Chilies

Tex-Mex Tostadas

4 (8-inch) fat-free flour tortillas
Nonstick cooking spray
1 green bell pepper, diced
¾ pound boneless skinless chicken breast, cut into strips
1½ teaspoons fresh or bottled minced garlic
1 teaspoon chili powder
1 teaspoon ground cumin
½ cup chunky salsa, divided
⅓ cup sliced green onions
1 cup canned fat-free refried beans
1 medium tomato, diced
¼ cup fat-free or reduced-fat sour cream (optional)

1. Preheat oven to 450°F. Place tortillas on baking sheet; coat both sides with cooking spray. Bake 5 minutes or until lightly browned and crisp. Remove; set aside.

2. Coat large nonstick skillet with cooking spray. Add bell pepper; cook and stir 4 minutes. Add chicken, garlic, chili powder and cumin; cook and stir 4 minutes or until chicken is no longer pink in center. Add ¼ cup salsa and green onions; cook and stir 1 minute. Remove skillet from heat; set aside.

3. Combine refried beans and remaining ¼ cup salsa in microwavable bowl. Cook uncovered at HIGH 1½ minutes or until beans are heated through.

4. Spread bean mixture evenly over tortillas. Spoon chicken mixture and tomato over bean mixture. Garnish with sour cream, if desired. *Makes 4 servings*

Tex-Mex Tostada

Chipotle Tamale Pie

¾ **pound ground turkey breast or lean ground beef**
1 **cup chopped onion**
¾ **cup diced green bell pepper**
¾ **cup diced red bell pepper**
4 **cloves garlic, minced**
2 **teaspoons ground cumin**
1 **can (15 ounces) pinto or red beans, rinsed and drained**
1 **can (8 ounces) no-salt-added stewed tomatoes, undrained**
2 **canned chipotle chilies in adobo sauce, minced (about 1 tablespoon)**
1 **to 2 teaspoons adobo sauce from canned chilies (optional)**
1 **cup (4 ounces) reduced-fat shredded Cheddar cheese**
½ **cup chopped fresh cilantro**
1 **package (8½ ounces) corn bread mix**
⅓ **cup low-fat (1%) milk**
1 **large egg white**

1. Preheat oven to 400°F.

2. Cook turkey, onion, bell peppers and garlic in large nonstick skillet over medium-high heat 8 minutes or until turkey is no longer pink, stirring occasionally. Drain fat; sprinkle mixture with cumin.

3. Add beans, tomatoes, chilies and adobo sauce; bring to a boil over high heat. Reduce heat to medium; simmer, uncovered, 5 minutes. Remove from heat; stir in cheese and cilantro.

4. Spray 8-inch square baking dish with nonstick cooking spray. Spoon turkey mixture evenly into prepared dish, pressing down to compact mixture. Combine corn bread mix, milk and egg white in medium bowl; mix just until dry ingredients are moistened. Spoon batter evenly over turkey mixture to cover completely.

5. Bake 20 to 22 minutes or until corn bread is golden brown. Let stand 5 minutes before serving.

Makes 6 servings

Chipotle Tamale Pie

Chile Verde

½ to ¾ pound boneless lean pork
1 large onion, halved and thinly sliced
4 cloves garlic, chopped or sliced
½ cup water
1 pound fresh tomatillos
1 can (14½ ounces) ⅓-less-salt chicken broth
1 can (4 ounces) diced mild green chilies
1 teaspoon ground cumin
1½ cups cooked navy or Great Northern beans, *or* 1 can (15 ounces) Great Northern beans, rinsed and drained
½ cup lightly packed fresh cilantro, chopped
Nonfat plain yogurt (optional)

1. Trim fat from pork; discard. Cut meat into ¾- to 1-inch cubes. Place pork, onion, garlic and water into large saucepan. Cover; simmer over medium-low heat, stirring occasionally, 30 minutes (add more water if necessary). Uncover; boil over medium-high heat until liquid evaporates and meat browns.

2. Add tomatillos and broth; stir. Cover; simmer over medium heat 20 minutes or until tomatillos are tender. Tear tomatillos apart with 2 forks. Add chilies and cumin. Cover; simmer over medium-low heat 45 minutes or until meat is tender and tears apart easily (add more water or broth to keep liquid level the same). Add beans; simmer 10 minutes or until heated through. Stir in cilantro. Serve with yogurt, if desired.   *Makes 4 servings*

Chile Verde

Tex-Mex Chicken

1 teaspoon ground red pepper
¾ teaspoon onion powder
¾ teaspoon garlic powder
½ teaspoon salt, divided
½ teaspoon dried basil leaves
⅛ teaspoon dried oregano leaves
⅛ teaspoon dried thyme leaves
⅛ teaspoon gumbo file powder* (optional)
6 boneless skinless chicken breast halves (1½ pounds)
¾ pound potatoes, cut into 1-inch wedges
Nonstick cooking spray
¼ teaspoon black pepper

*Gumbo file powder is a seasoning widely used in Creole cooking. It is available in the spice or gourmet section of most large supermarkets.

1. Combine red pepper, onion powder, garlic powder, ¼ teaspoon salt, basil, oregano, thyme and file powder, if desired, in small bowl. Rub mixture on all surfaces of chicken. Place chicken in single layer in 13×9-inch baking pan. Refrigerate, covered, 4 to 8 hours.

2. Preheat oven to 350°F. Place potatoes in medium bowl. Spray potatoes lightly with cooking spray; toss to coat. Sprinkle with remaining ¼ teaspoon salt and black pepper; toss to combine. Add to chicken in pan.

3. Bake, uncovered, 40 to 45 minutes or until potatoes are tender and chicken is no longer pink in center. Or, grill chicken and potatoes, in foil pan, on covered grill over medium-hot coals, 20 to 30 minutes or until potatoes are tender and chicken is no longer pink in center. Serve with additional vegetables, if desired. *Makes 6 servings*

Festive Skillet Fajitas

1½ pounds boneless, skinless chicken breasts, cut into ½-inch strips
1 medium onion, cut into thin wedges
2 cloves garlic, minced
1 tablespoon vegetable oil
½ teaspoon ground cumin
1 can (14½ ounces) DEL MONTE® Zesty Diced Tomatoes with Jalapeño Peppers
1 can (7 ounces) whole green chiles, drained and cut into strips
8 flour tortillas, warmed

1. Brown chicken with onion and garlic in oil in large skillet over medium-high heat.

2. Stir in cumin, tomatoes and chiles; heat through.

3. Fill warmed tortillas with chicken mixture. Garnish with sour cream, avocado or guacamole, cilantro and lime wedges, if desired. Serve immediately.   *Makes 6 to 8 servings*

Prep Time: 10 minutes
Cook Time: 10 minutes

Red Snapper Vera Cruz

4 red snapper fillets (1 pound)
¼ cup fresh lime juice
1 tablespoon fresh lemon juice
1 teaspoon chili powder
4 green onions with 4 inches of tops, sliced in ½-inch lengths
1 tomato, coarsely chopped
½ cup chopped Anaheim or green bell pepper
½ cup chopped red bell pepper

1. Place red snapper in shallow round microwavable baking dish. Combine lime juice, lemon juice and chili powder. Pour over snapper. Marinate 10 minutes, turning once or twice.

2. Sprinkle green onions, tomato and peppers over snapper. Cover dish loosely with vented plastic wrap. Microwave at HIGH 6 minutes or just until snapper flakes in center, rotating dish every 2 minutes. Let stand, covered, 4 minutes.   *Makes 4 servings*

Stuffed Bell Peppers

1 package (8½ ounces) cornbread mix *plus* ingredients for preparation
6 green bell peppers
1 large onion, thinly sliced
1 teaspoon olive oil
1 can (16 ounces) no-salt-added diced tomatoes
1 package (10 ounces) frozen corn, thawed and drained
1 can (2¼ ounces) sliced black olives, drained
⅓ cup raisins
1 tablespoon chili powder
1 teaspoon ground sage
1 cup (4 ounces) shredded reduced-fat Monterey Jack cheese, divided
Cherry tomato halves and fresh herbs for garnish

Prepare cornbread according to package directions. Cut into cubes. *Reduce oven temperature to 350°F.* Slice tops off peppers; discard stems and seeds. Finely chop tops to equal 1 cup; set aside. Rinse peppers. Bring 2 to 3 inches water to a boil over high heat in large saucepan. Add 1 or more peppers and boil 1 minute, turning peppers with tongs to blanch evenly. Rinse with cold water; drain. Repeat with remaining peppers.

Place onion and oil in Dutch oven. Cover and cook over medium-high heat, stirring occasionally, 8 to 10 minutes or until onion is tender and browned. Add 1 to 2 tablespoons water, if needed, to prevent sticking. Add chopped pepper; stir 1 minute more. Remove from heat. Add tomatoes, corn, olives, raisins, chili powder and sage; stir. Stir in corn bread (it will crumble) and ¾ cup cheese. Spoon filling into peppers. Top with remaining ¼ cup cheese. Place peppers in baking dish; bake 20 to 30 minutes or until heated through. Garnish, if desired. *Makes 6 servings*

Stuffed Bell Pepper

Sassy Chicken & Peppers

2 teaspoons Mexican seasoning*
2 (4-ounce) boneless skinless chicken breasts
2 teaspoons canola oil
1 small red onion, sliced
½ red bell pepper, cut into long thin strips
½ yellow or green bell pepper, cut into long thin strips
¼ cup chunky salsa or chipotle salsa
1 tablespoon lime juice
   Lime wedges (optional)

*If Mexican seasoning is not available, substitute 1 teaspoon chili powder, ½ teaspoon ground cumin, ½ teaspoon salt and ⅛ teaspoon ground red pepper.

1. Sprinkle seasoning over both sides of chicken.

2. Heat oil in large nonstick skillet over medium heat. Add onion; cook 3 minutes, stirring occasionally.

3. Add bell pepper strips; cook 3 minutes, stirring occasionally.

4. Push vegetables to edges of skillet; add chicken to skillet. Cook 5 minutes; turn. Stir salsa and lime juice into vegetables. Continue to cook 4 minutes or until chicken is no longer pink in the center and vegetables are tender.

5. Transfer chicken to serving plates; top with vegetable mixture and garnish with lime wedges, if desired.
Makes 2 servings

Sassy Chicken & Peppers

Turkey Ham Quesadillas

¼ **cup picante sauce or salsa**
 4 **(7-inch) regular or whole wheat flour tortillas**
½ **cup shredded reduced-fat Monterey Jack cheese**
¼ **cup finely chopped turkey ham or lean ham**
¼ **cup canned green chilies, drained** *or* **1 to 2 tablespoons chopped fresh jalapeño peppers***
   to taste
   Nonstick cooking spray
   Additional picante sauce or salsa for dipping (optional)
   Fat-free or low-fat sour cream (optional)

*Jalapeño peppers can sting and irritate the skin; wear rubber gloves when handling peppers and do not touch eyes. Wash hands after handling.

1. Spread 1 tablespoon picante sauce on each tortilla.

2. Sprinkle cheese, turkey ham and chilies equally over half of each tortilla. Fold over uncovered half to make quesadilla; spray tops and bottoms of quesadillas with cooking spray.

3. Grill on uncovered grill over medium coals 1½ minutes per side or until cheese is melted and tortillas are golden brown, turning once. Quarter each quesadilla and serve with additional picante sauce and fat-free sour cream, if desired. *Makes 2 servings*

Turkey Ham Quesadillas

Side Dishes

South-of-the-Border Vegetable Kabobs

> 5 cloves garlic, peeled
> $\frac{1}{2}$ cup A.1.® BOLD & SPICY Steak Sauce
> $\frac{1}{4}$ cup butter or margarine, melted
> 1 tablespoon finely chopped cilantro
> $\frac{3}{4}$ teaspoon ground cumin
> $\frac{1}{4}$ teaspoon coarsely ground black pepper
> $\frac{1}{8}$ teaspoon ground red pepper
> 3 ears corn, cut crosswise into 1$\frac{1}{2}$-inch slices and blanched
> 3 medium plum tomatoes, cut into $\frac{1}{2}$-inch slices
> 1 small zucchini, cut lengthwise into thin slices
> 1 cup baby carrots, blanched

1. Mince 1 garlic clove; halve remaining garlic cloves and set aside. Blend steak sauce, butter, cilantro, minced garlic, cumin and peppers in small bowl; set aside.

2. Alternately thread vegetables and halved garlic cloves onto 6 (10-inch) metal skewers.

3. Grill kabobs over medium heat for 7 to 9 minutes or until done, turning and basting often with steak sauce mixture. Remove from skewers; serve immediately.   *Makes 6 servings*

South-of-the-Border Vegetable Kabobs

Cimarron Slaw

2 cups finely shredded green cabbage
2 cups finely shredded red cabbage
1 cup jicama strips
¼ cup diced green bell pepper
¼ cup thinly sliced green onions with tops
¼ cup vegetable oil
¼ cup lime juice
¾ teaspoon salt
⅛ teaspoon black pepper
2 tablespoons coarsely chopped fresh cilantro

Combine cabbages, jicama, bell pepper and green onions in large bowl. Whisk oil, lime juice, salt and black pepper in small bowl until well blended. Stir in cilantro. Pour over cabbage mixture; toss lightly. Cover; refrigerate 2 hours or up to 6 hours for flavors to blend. *Makes 4 to 6 servings*

Corn Maque Choux

2 tablespoons butter *or* margarine
½ cup chopped onion
½ cup chopped green pepper
4 cups whole kernel corn (canned, fresh or frozen, thawed)
1 medium tomato, chopped
¼ teaspoon salt
½ teaspoon TABASCO® brand Pepper Sauce

Melt butter over medium heat in 3-quart saucepan.

Add onion and green pepper; cook 5 minutes or until tender, stirring frequently.

Stir in corn, tomato, salt and TABASCO® Sauce.

Reduce heat and simmer 10 to 15 minutes or until corn is tender. *Makes 3 cups*

*Top to bottom: Cimarron Slaw and
Three Bean Salad
with Nopalitos (page 304)*

Three Bean Salad with Nopalitos

1 can (17 ounces) green lima beans, drained
1 can (15½ ounces) garbanzo beans, drained
1 can (15½ ounces) kidney beans, drained
1 cup canned nopalitos, drained
1 cup thinly sliced celery
¼ cup thinly sliced green onions with tops
½ cup olive oil
3 tablespoons sherry wine vinegar or red wine vinegar
1 teaspoon grated lemon peel
1 teaspoon lemon juice
¾ teaspoon salt
½ teaspoon paprika
¼ teaspoon black pepper
¼ cup chopped fresh parsley

Combine beans, nopalitos, celery and green onions in large bowl. Whisk oil, vinegar, lemon peel, lemon juice, salt, paprika and pepper in small bowl until well blended; stir in parsley. Pour over bean mixture; toss gently until vegetables are well coated. Cover; refrigerate 2 hours or overnight for flavors to blend.

Makes 6 to 8 servings

Señor Says: **Nopalitos are diced or strips of a prickly pear cactus. This popular Mexican food is available canned in Mexican markets and large supermarkets.**

Chili Bean Del Monte®

¾ cup sliced green onions, divided
1 can (15 ounces) pinto beans, drained
1 can (14½ ounces) DEL MONTE® Zesty Chili Style Chunky Tomatoes
1 can (8¾ ounces) *or* 1 cup kidney beans, drained
½ to 1 teaspoon minced jalapeño pepper*
½ teaspoon ground cumin
¼ teaspoon garlic powder
¼ cup shredded sharp Cheddar cheese

*Jalapeño peppers can sting and irritate the skin; wear rubber gloves when handling peppers and do not touch eyes. Wash hands after handling peppers.

1. Set aside ¼ cup green onions for garnish. In large skillet, combine remaining ½ cup green onions with remaining ingredients except cheese.

2. Bring to a boil; reduce heat to medium. Cook 5 minutes. Serve with cheese and reserved onions.

Makes 3 servings (approximately ¾ cup each)

Frijoles Rancheros

4 bacon slices, chopped
1 medium onion, chopped
1 red bell pepper, chopped
1 can (16 ounces) refried beans
1 can (16 ounces) pinto or pink beans, drained
⅓ cup chopped chives
¼ cup biscuit mix
½ teaspoon LAWRY'S® Seasoned Pepper
¼ teaspoon LAWRY'S® Garlic Powder with Parsley
¼ teaspoon hot pepper sauce
3 slices cheddar or jalapeño pepper cheese

In medium skillet, cook bacon, onion and bell pepper over medium-high heat until bacon is browned and vegetables are tender, about 7 minutes. Stir in remaining ingredients except cheese. Pour into 1½-quart baking dish. Top with cheese. Bake in 375°F oven 20 minutes or until cheese melts. Let stand 2 minutes before serving.

Makes 6 servings

Colache

2 tablespoons vegetable oil
1 butternut squash (about 2 pounds) peeled, seeded and diced
1 medium onion, coarsely chopped
1 clove garlic, minced
1 can (16 ounces) tomatoes, undrained
1 green bell pepper, seeded and cut into 1-inch pieces
1 can (14½ ounces) whole kernel corn, drained
1 canned green chili, coarsely chopped (optional)
½ teaspoon salt
¼ teaspoon black pepper

Heat oil in large skillet over medium heat. Add squash, onion and garlic; cook 5 minutes or until onion is tender. Coarsely cut up tomatoes; add tomatoes and bell pepper to skillet. Bring to a boil over high heat. Cover; reduce heat and simmer 15 minutes. Add remaining ingredients. Simmer, covered, 5 minutes or until squash is tender. Uncover; increase heat to high. Continue cooking a few minutes or until most of liquid has evaporated. *Makes 6 to 8 servings*

Mexicali Corn

1 tablespoon butter or margarine
1½ cups chopped onion and bell pepper
1 package (16 ounces) frozen whole kernel corn
⅛ teaspoon garlic powder
3 tablespoons *Frank's® RedHot®* Cayenne Pepper Sauce

1. Melt butter in saucepan over medium-high heat. Cook and stir onion and peppers in butter until crisp-tender. Stir in corn and garlic powder.

2. Cover pan; cook over medium heat 3 minutes until corn is tender. Stir in **Frank's RedHot** Sauce.
Makes 4 to 6 servings

Prep Time: 5 minutes
Cook Time: 8 minutes

Colache

Mexican Rice

2 tablespoons butter or margarine
1 cup long-grain white rice
½ cup chopped onion
2 cloves garlic, finely chopped
1 jar (16 ounces) ORTEGA® Salsa Prima-Thick & Chunky
¾ cup (1 large) peeled, shredded carrot
½ cup frozen peas, thawed (optional)

MELT butter in large saucepan over medium heat. Add rice, onion and garlic; cook, stirring occasionally, for 3 to 4 minutes or until rice is golden. Stir in salsa, water, carrot and peas. Bring to a boil. Reduce heat to low; cook, covered, for 25 to 30 minutes or until liquid is absorbed and rice is tender.

Makes 8 servings

Señor Says: For a quick-cook Mexican Rice, use 4 cups instant rice instead of 1 cup long-grain white rice, and 2½ cups water instead of 1¼ cups water. After salsa mixture comes to a boil, cook for a length of time recommended on instant rice package.

Mexican Rice

"Wild" Black Beans

2 cups cooked wild rice
1 can (15 ounces) black beans, undrained
1 cup canned or thawed frozen corn, drained
½ cup chopped red bell pepper
1 small jalapeño pepper, seeded and chopped*
1 tablespoon red wine vinegar
1 cup (4 ounces) shredded Monterey Jack cheese
¼ cup chopped fresh cilantro

*Jalapeño peppers can sting and irritate the skin; wear rubber gloves when handling peppers and do not touch eyes. Wash hands after handling peppers.

Preheat oven to 350°F. In 1½-quart baking dish, combine wild rice, beans, corn, bell pepper, jalapeño pepper and vinegar. Cover; bake 20 minutes. Top with cheese; bake, uncovered, 10 minutes. Garnish with cilantro. *Makes 6 to 8 servings*

Favorite recipe from **Minnesota Cultivated Wild Rice Council**

Mexican Corn Custard Bake

1 can (11 ounces) Mexican-style whole kernel corn, drained
¼ cup all-purpose flour
1 jar (16 ounces) chunky medium salsa, divided
5 eggs, beaten
½ cup sour cream
1⅓ cups *French's*® French Fried Onions, divided
1 cup (4 ounces) shredded Monterey Jack cheese with jalapeño peppers or Cheddar cheese

Preheat oven to 375°F. Grease 9-inch deep-dish pie plate. Combine corn and flour in large bowl. Stir in ¾ cup salsa, eggs, sour cream and ⅔ *cup* French Fried Onions; mix until well blended. Pour into prepared pie plate. Cover; bake 45 minutes or until custard is set.

Pour remaining salsa around edge of dish. Sprinkle with cheese and remaining ⅔ *cup* onions. Bake, uncovered, 3 minutes or until onions are golden. Cut into wedges to serve. *Makes 6 servings*

Picante Pintos and Rice

  2 cups dried pinto beans
  2 cups water
  1 can (14½ ounces) no-salt-added stewed tomatoes
  1 cup coarsely chopped onion
  ¾ cup coarsely chopped green bell pepper
  ¼ cup sliced celery
  4 cloves garlic, minced
  ½ small jalapeño pepper,* seeded and chopped
  2 teaspoons dried oregano leaves
  2 teaspoons chili powder
  ½ teaspoon ground red pepper
  2 cups chopped kale
  3 cups cooked rice

*Jalapeño peppers can sting and irritate the skin; wear rubber gloves when handling peppers and do not touch eyes. Wash hands after handling peppers.

Place beans in large saucepan; add water to cover beans by 2 inches. Bring to a boil over high heat; boil 2 minutes. Remove pan from heat; let stand, covered, 1 hour. Drain beans; discard water. Return to saucepan.

Add 2 cups water, tomatoes, onion, bell pepper, celery, garlic, jalapeño pepper, oregano, chili powder and ground red pepper to saucepan; bring to a boil over high heat. Reduce heat to low. Simmer, covered, about 1½ hours or until beans are tender, stirring occasionally.

Gently stir kale into bean mixture. Simmer, uncovered, 30 minutes. (Beans will be very tender and mixture will have consistency of thick sauce.) Serve over rice.   *Makes 6 servings*

Green Rice Pilaf

2 tablespoons vegetable oil
1 cup uncooked long-grain white rice (not converted)
¼ cup finely chopped white onion
2 fresh poblano or Anaheim chilies, roasted, peeled, seeded, deveined and chopped*
6 thin green onions, thinly sliced
1 clove garlic, minced
¼ teaspoon salt
¼ teaspoon ground cumin
1¾ cups chicken broth
1½ cups shredded queso Chihuahua or Monterey Jack cheese, divided
⅓ cup coarsely chopped fresh cilantro
Cilantro sprig for garnish

*Poblano peppers can sting and irritate the skin; wear rubber gloves when handling peppers and do not touch eyes. Wash hands after handling peppers.

1. Preheat oven to 375°F. Heat oil in large skillet over medium heat until hot. Add rice. Cook and stir 2 minutes or until rice turns opaque.

2. Add white onion; cook and stir 1 minute. Stir in chilies, green onions, garlic, salt and cumin; cook and stir 20 seconds.

3. Stir in broth. Bring to a boil over high heat. Reduce heat to low. Cover and simmer 15 minutes or until rice is almost tender.**

4. Remove skillet from heat. Add 1 cup cheese and chopped cilantro; toss lightly to mix. Transfer to greased 1½-quart baking dish; top with remaining ½ cup cheese.

5. Bake, uncovered, 15 minutes or until rice is tender and cheese topping is melted. Garnish, if desired.   *Makes 4 to 6 servings*

**For plain green rice, complete recipe from this point as follows: Cook rice in skillet 2 to 4 minutes more until tender. Stir in chopped cilantro just before serving; omit cheese.

Green Rice Pilaf

Arroz Blanco

1 tablespoon margarine
½ cup chopped onion
2 cloves garlic, minced
1 cup uncooked rice*
2 cups chicken broth

*Recipe based on regular-milled long grain white rice.

Melt margarine in 2- to 3-quart saucepan over medium heat. Add onion and garlic; cook until onion is tender. Add rice and broth. Bring to a boil; stir. Reduce heat; cover and simmer 15 minutes or until rice is tender and liquid is absorbed. Fluff with fork.

Makes 6 servings

To microwave: Combine margarine, onion, and garlic in deep 2- to 3-quart microproof baking dish. Cover and cook on HIGH 2 minutes. Stir in rice and broth; cover and cook on HIGH 5 minutes. Reduce setting to MEDIUM (50% power) and cook 15 minutes or until rice is tender and liquid is absorbed. Let stand 5 minutes. Fluff with fork.

Tip: Prepare a double batch of Arroz Blanco to have one batch ready for Rice with Tomato and Chiles or Green Rice (page 316) later in the week.

Favorite recipe from **USA Rice Federation**

Clockwise from top: Arroz Blanco, Rice with Tomato and Chiles and Green Rice (page 316)

Green Rice

> **2 Anaheim chilies***
> **1 jalapeño pepper***
> **1 tablespoon margarine or olive oil**
> **¼ cup sliced green onions**
> **¼ cup snipped cilantro**
> **1 recipe Arroz Blanco (recipe page 314)**
> **¼ teaspoon dried oregano leaves**
>
> *Anaheim chilies and jalapeño peppers can sting and irritate the skin; wear rubber gloves when handling peppers and do not touch eyes. Wash hands after handling peppers.

Chop chilies and jalapeño pepper in food processor until minced, but not liquefied. Melt margarine in large skillet over low heat. Add chilies mixture; cook 1 minute over medium heat. Stir in onions and cilantro; cook 15 to 30 seconds. Add Arroz Blanco and oregano; heat. *Makes 6 servings*

Favorite recipe from **USA Rice Federation**

Rice with Tomato and Chiles

> **1 green pepper, diced**
> **½ cup chopped onion**
> **1 jalapeño pepper*, chopped**
> **1 tablespoon olive oil**
> **1 recipe Arroz Blanco (recipe page 314)**
> **1 can (14½ ounces) whole tomatoes, drained and chopped**
> **⅛ teaspoon dried oregano leaves**
> **2 tablespoons snipped cilantro for garnish**
>
> *Jalapeño peppers can sting and irritate the skin; wear rubber gloves when handling peppers and do not touch eyes. Wash hands after handling peppers.

Cook green pepper, onion, and jalapeño pepper in oil in large skillet over medium-high heat until tender crisp. Stir in Arroz Blanco, tomatoes, and oregano; cook 5 minutes longer. Garnish with cilantro. *Makes 6 servings*

Favorite recipe from **USA Rice Federation**

Grilled Green Chile & Cheddar Stuffed Potatoes

4 medium baking potatoes, scrubbed
1 tablespoon olive oil
$\frac{1}{3}$ cup reduced-fat sour cream
$\frac{1}{4}$ cup low-fat milk
1 can (4 ounces) diced green chiles, drained
$\frac{3}{4}$ teaspoon salt
$\frac{1}{8}$ teaspoon black pepper
$\frac{3}{4}$ cup (3 ounces) shredded Cheddar cheese, divided

Preheat oven to 400°F. Pierce potatoes with fork several times. Bake 1 hour until tender. Cool slightly; cut lengthwise into halves. Scoop out potato pulp with spoon, leaving $\frac{1}{4}$-inch shell. Place pulp in medium bowl. Brush outsides of shells with oil; set aside. Whip or mash potato pulp with sour cream and milk until smooth. Stir in chiles, salt, pepper and $\frac{1}{2}$ cup cheese. Carefully spoon potato mixture into shells. Top with remaining $\frac{1}{4}$ cup cheese. Grill potatoes on covered grill over medium KINGSFORD® Briquets 8 to 10 minutes or until heated through. *Makes 8 servings*

Microwave Directions: Pierce potatoes; place on paper towel in microwave oven. Microwave at HIGH 5 minutes. Turn and microwave at HIGH 4 minutes until tender. Complete recipe as directed above.

Potato Skins: Bake potatoes and scoop out pulp as directed above. Save removed potato pulp for another use. Omit oil; use palm of hand to flatten skins. Brush skins, inside and out, with 2 tablespoons melted butter; sprinkle with salt and pepper. Grill potato skins, cut side down, on covered grill over medium Kingsford® briquets 2 to 3 minutes or until lightly browned. Turn potato skins; top with Cheddar cheese. Grill until lightly browned and cheese is melted. Serve immediately.

Blue Cheese Skins: Prepare as directed for Potato Skins. Substitute 1 cup crumbled blue cheese for Cheddar cheese.

Nacho Skins: Prepare as directed for Potato Skins. Increase Cheddar cheese to 1 cup (or substitute 1 cup Monterey Jack cheese). Before serving, top each potato skin with 2 tablespoons *each* reduced-fat sour cream and fresh salsa.

Sombrero Vegetable Bake

1 tablespoon olive oil

1 clove garlic, minced

¼ teaspoon ground cumin

1 can (14½ ounces) stewed tomatoes

1 package (9 ounces) frozen corn, thawed

2 small zucchini, cut into ¾-inch chunks

2 tablespoons *Frank's® RedHot®* Cayenne Pepper Sauce

¼ teaspoon salt

1⅓ cups *French's®* French Fried Onions

Whisk together oil, garlic and cumin in 2-quart microwavable bowl. Microwave, uncovered, at HIGH 1 minute.

Stir in tomatoes with liquid, corn, zucchini, **Frank's RedHot** Sauce and salt. Cover tightly with plastic wrap. Microwave at HIGH 8 to 10 minutes or until zucchini is crisp-tender, stirring twice. Uncover; sprinkle with French Fried Onions. Microwave on HIGH 1 minute or until onions are golden.

Makes 6 side-dish servings

Prep Time: 10 minutes
Cook Time: 12 minutes

Confetti Black Beans

1 cup dried black beans
3 cups water
1 can (14 ounces) reduced-sodium chicken broth
1 bay leaf
1½ teaspoons olive oil
1 medium onion, chopped
¼ cup chopped red bell pepper
¼ cup chopped yellow bell pepper
2 cloves garlic, minced
1 jalapeño pepper,* finely chopped
1 large tomato, seeded and chopped
½ teaspoon salt
⅛ teaspoon black pepper
Hot pepper sauce (optional)

*Jalapeño peppers can sting and irritate the skin; wear rubber gloves when handling peppers and do not touch eyes. Wash hands after handling peppers.

1. Sort and rinse black beans. Cover with water and soak overnight; drain. Place beans in large saucepan with chicken broth; bring to a boil over high heat. Add bay leaf. Reduce heat to low; cover and simmer about 1½ hours or until beans are tender.

2. Heat oil in large skillet over medium heat. Add onion, bell peppers, garlic and jalapeño pepper; cook 8 to 10 minutes or until onion is tender, stirring frequently. Add tomato, salt and black pepper; cook 5 minutes.

3. Add onion mixture to beans; cook 15 to 20 minutes. Remove bay leaf before serving. Serve with hot sauce and garnish, if desired.

Makes 6 servings

Confetti Black Beans

Hot Mexican Bean and Rice Salad

    1 bag SUCCESS® Rice
    2 tablespoons reduced-calorie margarine
    ½ cup chopped onion
    ¼ cup chopped green bell pepper
    ½ teaspoon ground cumin
    2 low-sodium chicken bouillon cubes, crushed
    ¼ cup water
    ¼ teaspoon salt
    ¼ teaspoon black pepper
    1 can (15½ ounces) kidney beans, drained
    ¼ cup chopped pimentos

Prepare rice according to package directions.

Melt margarine in medium saucepan over medium heat. Add onion, green pepper and cumin; cook and stir until vegetables are crisp-tender. Add bouillon cubes, water, salt and black pepper. Bring to a boil. Add rice, beans and pimentos. Reduce heat to low; heat thoroughly, stirring occasionally.

Makes 8 servings

Sour Cream Tortilla Casserole

    2 tablespoons vegetable oil
    ½ cup chopped onion
    1 can (28 ounces) whole tomatoes, cut up
    ¼ cup chunky salsa
    1 package (1.0 ounce) LAWRY'S® Taco Spices & Seasonings
    12 corn tortillas
      Vegetable oil
    ¾ cup chopped onion
    4 cups (16 ounces) shredded Monterey Jack cheese
    1½ cups dairy sour cream
      LAWRY'S® Seasoned Pepper

In medium skillet, heat 2 tablespoons oil. Add ½ cup onion and cook over medium-high heat until tender. Add tomatoes, salsa and Taco Spices & Seasonings. Bring to a boil over medium-high heat; reduce heat to low and simmer, uncovered, 15 minutes. In small skillet, fry tortillas lightly, one at a time, in small amount of oil, 10 to 15 seconds on each side. In bottom of 13×9×2-inch baking dish, pour ½ cup sauce. Arrange layer of tortillas over sauce; top with ⅓ of sauce, onion and cheese. Repeat layers 2 times. Spread sour cream over cheese. Sprinkle lightly with Seasoned Pepper. Bake in 325°F oven 25 to 30 minutes.

Makes 10 to 12 servings

Serving Suggestion: Cut into squares.

Hint: LAWRY'S® Spices & Seasonings for Chili may be substituted for Taco Spices & Seasonings. For fewer calories, do not fry tortillas.

Mexican Braised Celery

6 medium to large ribs celery
1 can (14½ ounces) no-salt-added stewed tomatoes, undrained
2 cloves garlic, minced
¼ teaspoon ground cumin
1 cup frozen whole kernel corn, thawed
¾ cup chopped green bell pepper
½ cup finely chopped onion
1 tablespoon minced seeded jalapeño pepper*
2 tablespoons minced fresh cilantro

*Jalapeño peppers can sting and irritate the skin; wear rubber gloves when handling peppers and do not touch eyes. Wash hands after handling peppers.

Trim off ends and remove strings from celery; cut into 2-inch lengths. Place celery in single layer in large skillet. Add tomatoes with juice (breaking up large pieces), garlic and cumin; bring to a boil over high heat. Reduce heat to low. Simmer, covered, 10 minutes.

Combine corn, bell pepper, onion and jalapeño pepper in small bowl; sprinkle evenly over celery mixture. Simmer, covered, 10 to 12 minutes more or until celery is tender, stirring once. Serve in shallow bowls; sprinkle with cilantro before serving.

Makes 4 servings

Tex-Mex Quick Bread

1½ cups all-purpose flour
1 cup (4 ounces) shredded Monterey Jack cheese
½ cup cornmeal
½ cup sun-dried tomatoes, coarsely chopped
1 can (4¼ ounces) black olives, drained and chopped
¼ cup sugar
1½ teaspoons baking powder
1 teaspoon baking soda
1 cup milk
1 can (4½ ounces) green chilies, drained and chopped
¼ cup olive oil
1 large egg, beaten

1. Preheat oven to 325°F. Grease 9×5-inch loaf pan or four 5×3-inch loaf pans; set aside.

2. Combine flour, cheese, cornmeal, tomatoes, olives, sugar, baking powder and baking soda in large bowl.

3. Combine remaining ingredients in small bowl. Add to flour mixture; stir just until combined. Pour into prepared pan. Bake 9×5-inch loaf 45 minutes and 5×3-inch loaves 30 minutes or until toothpick inserted near center of loaf comes out clean. Cool in pan 15 minutes. Remove from pan and cool on wire rack.   *Makes 1 large loaf or 4 small loaves*

Muffin Variation: Preheat oven to 375°F. Spoon batter into 12 well-greased muffin cups. Bake 20 minutes or until toothpick inserted near center of muffin comes out clean. Makes 12 muffins.

Spicy Southwestern Vegetables

1 bag (16 ounces) frozen green beans
2 tablespoons water
1 tablespoon olive oil
1 red bell pepper, chopped
1 medium yellow summer squash or zucchini, chopped
1 jalapeño pepper,* seeded, and chopped (optional)
½ teaspoon ground cumin
½ teaspoon garlic powder
½ teaspoon chili powder
¼ cup sliced green onions
2 tablespoons chopped fresh cilantro (optional)
1 tablespoon brown sugar

*Jalapeños can sting and irritate the skin; wear rubber gloves when handling peppers and do not touch eyes. Wash hands after handling peppers.

1. Heat large skillet over medium heat; add green beans, water and oil. Cover; cook 4 minutes, stirring occasionally.

2. Add bell pepper, squash, jalapeño pepper, if desired, cumin, garlic powder and chili powder. Cook, uncovered, stirring occasionally, 4 minutes or until vegetables are crisp-tender. Stir in green onions, cilantro, if desired, and brown sugar. *Makes 6 servings*

Spicy Southwestern Vegetables

South-of-the-Border "Baked" Beans

½ cup KARO® Light or Dark Corn Syrup
¼ cup ketchup
1 tablespoon cider vinegar
1 teaspoon chili powder
½ teaspoon salt
2 cans (16 ounces each) kidney or black beans, rinsed and drained
1 can (12 ounces) kernel corn, drained
1 can (4 ounces) chopped green chilies, drained, *or* 1 tablespoon seeded and chopped jalapeño pepper*
½ cup finely chopped onion

*Wear rubber gloves when working with hot peppers or wash hands in warm soapy water after handling. Avoid touching face or eyes.

MICROWAVE DIRECTIONS

1. In 1½-quart microwavable casserole combine corn syrup, ketchup, vinegar, chili powder and salt. Stir in beans, corn, chilies and onion.

2. Microwave on HIGH (100%), 15 minutes or until hot and bubbly, stirring twice. Let stand 5 minutes before serving.   *Makes 6 servings*

Prep Time: 35 minutes

Zucchini Mexicana

1 tablespoon vegetable oil
1 medium onion, thinly sliced
1½ pounds zucchini, thinly sliced
1 can (14½ ounces) whole peeled tomatoes, drained and cut up
2 tablespoons chopped green chiles
1 teaspoon LAWRY'S® Seasoned Salt
¾ teaspoon LAWRY'S® Garlic Powder with Parsley
½ teaspoon LAWRY'S® Seasoned Pepper
1 cup (4 ounces) shredded Monterey Jack cheese

In medium skillet, heat oil. Add onion and cook over medium-high heat until tender. Add remaining ingredients except cheese. Bring to a boil over medium-high heat; reduce heat to low and simmer, uncovered, 5 to 10 minutes. Place zucchini mixture in 8-inch square baking dish and top with cheese. Bake, uncovered, in 375°F oven 10 minutes or until cheese melts.   *Makes 6 to 8 servings*

Serving Suggestion: Serve as a side dish with other Mexican specialties.

Salsa Rice and Black Beans

1¼ cups water
1½ cups MINUTE® Brown Rice, uncooked
1 can (16 ounces) black beans, rinsed, drained
1 large tomato, chopped
1 can (4 ounces) chopped green chilies, undrained
1 tablespoon chopped cilantro or fresh parsley
1 tablespoon lime juice
⅛ teaspoon hot pepper sauce
    Suggested garnishes: light sour cream, lime slices, cilantro or fresh parsley

BRING water to a boil in large saucepan over medium-high heat.

STIR in rice, beans, tomato and chilies. Return to boil. Reduce heat to low; cover and simmer 5 minutes. Remove from heat.

STIR in cilantro, lime juice and pepper sauce; cover. Let stand 5 minutes. Stir. Garnish as desired.
Makes 4 servings

Prep Time: 10 minutes
Cook Time: 20 Minutes

Desserts & More

Strawberry Margarita Pie

> 3 tablespoons margarine
> 2 tablespoons honey
> 1½ cups crushed pretzels
> 3 cups low-fat sugar-free strawberry frozen yogurt, softened
> 1½ cups thawed frozen light nondairy whipped topping
> 2 teaspoons grated lime peel, divided
> 1 package (16 ounces) strawberries in syrup, thawed
> 1 tablespoon lime juice
> 1 tablespoon tequila (optional)

1. Combine margarine and honey in medium microwavable bowl. Microwave at HIGH 30 seconds or until smooth when stirred. Add pretzels; stir until evenly coated. Press into bottom and side of 9-inch pie plate; freeze 30 minutes or until firm.

2. Combine frozen yogurt, whipped topping and 1 teaspoon lime peel in medium bowl; gently fold with rubber spatula. Spoon into pie plate. Freeze 2 hours or until firm.

3. Combine strawberries, lime juice and remaining 1 teaspoon peel in small bowl; stir to blend.

4. Cut pie into 8 portions; serve with strawberry mixture. Add tequila to strawberry mixture just before serving, if desired.

Makes 8 servings

Strawberry Margarita Pie

Caramel Flan

1 cup sugar, divided
2 cups half-and-half
1 cup milk
1½ teaspoons vanilla extract
6 eggs
2 egg yolks
Hot water
Fresh whole and sliced strawberries for garnish

1. Preheat oven to 325°F. Heat 5½- to 6-cup ring mold in oven 10 minutes or until hot.

2. Heat ½ cup sugar in heavy, medium skillet over medium-high heat 5 to 8 minutes or until sugar is completely melted and deep amber color, stirring frequently. *Do not allow sugar to burn.*

3. Immediately pour caramelized sugar into ring mold. Holding mold with potholder, quickly rotate to coat bottom and sides evenly with sugar. Place mold on wire rack. *Caution: Caramelized sugar is very hot; do not touch it.*

4. Combine half-and-half and milk in heavy 2-quart saucepan. Heat over medium heat until almost simmering; remove from heat. Add remaining ½ cup sugar and vanilla, stirring until sugar is dissolved.

5. Lightly beat eggs and egg yolks in large bowl until blended but not foamy; gradually stir in milk mixture. Pour custard into ring mold.

6. Place mold in large baking pan; pour hot water into baking pan to depth of ½ inch. Bake 35 to 40 minutes until knife inserted into center of custard comes out clean.

7. Remove mold from water bath; place on wire rack. Let stand 30 minutes. Cover and refrigerate 1½ to 2 hours until thoroughly chilled.

8. To serve, loosen inner and outer edges of flan with tip of small knife. Cover mold with rimmed serving plate; invert and lift off mold. Garnish, if desired. Spoon some of the melted caramel over each serving.

Makes 6 to 8 servings

Toasted Almond Horchata

3½ cups water, divided
2 (3-inch) cinnamon sticks
1 cup uncooked instant white rice
1 cup slivered almonds, toasted
3 cups cold water
¾ to 1 cup sugar
½ teaspoon vanilla
Lime wedges for garnish

Combine 3 cups water and cinnamon sticks in medium saucepan. Cover and bring to a boil over high heat. Reduce heat to medium-low. Simmer 15 minutes. Remove from heat; let cool to temperature of hot tap water. Measure cinnamon water to equal 3 cups, adding additional hot water if needed.

Place rice in food processor; process using on/off pulsing action 1 to 2 minutes or until rice is powdery. Add almonds; process until finely ground (mixture will begin to stick together). Remove rice mixture to medium bowl; stir in cinnamon water. Let stand 1 hour or until mixture is thick and rice grains are soft.

Remove cinnamon sticks; discard. Pour mixture into food processor. Add remaining ½ cup water; process 2 to 4 minutes or until mixture is very creamy. Strain mixture through fine-meshed sieve or several layers of dampened cheesecloth into half-gallon pitcher. Stir in 3 cups cold water, sugar and vanilla; stir until sugar is completely dissolved.

To serve, pour over ice cubes, if desired. Garnish, if desired.   *Makes 8 to 10 servings*

Toasted Almond Horchata

Dulce de Leche Frozen Dessert

> 3 cups half-and-half or milk
> 6 tablespoons KRAFT® Caramel Topping, divided
> 1 package (4-serving size) JELL-O® Butterscotch Flavor Instant Pudding & Pie Filling
> 1 package (4-serving size) JELL-O® Vanilla Flavor Instant Pudding & Pie Filling
> 1 tub (8 ounces) COOL WHIP® Whipped Topping, thawed

POUR half-and-half into large bowl. Stir in 2 tablespoons caramel topping until dissolved. Add pudding mixes. Beat with wire whisk 1 minute or until well blended. Gently stir in whipped topping until well mixed.

SPOON ½ of the pudding mixture into 8×4-inch loaf pan which has been lined with plastic wrap. Drizzle remaining caramel topping over mixture. Carefully spoon remaining pudding mixture over caramel and smooth with spatula.

FREEZE about 6 hours or overnight or until firm. Carefully invert pan onto serving platter and remove plastic wrap. Let stand at room temperature about 15 minutes before slicing.   *Makes 8 servings*

Variation: To prepare individual Dulce de Leche frozen pops or cups, spoon ½ of the pudding mixture into 10 to 12 paper-lined muffin cups. Place teaspoonful of caramel topping in center of each cup and cover with remaining pudding mixture. For pops, stick wooden popsicle sticks into each cup and freeze.

Prep Time: 20 minutes
Freeze Time: 6 hours

Mexican Coffee

> 6 cups hot brewed coffee
> 1 (14-ounce) can EAGLE® BRAND Sweetened Condensed Milk (NOT evaporated milk)
> ½ cup coffee liqueur
> 2 teaspoons vanilla extract
> ⅓ cup tequila, if desired
> Ground cinnamon, if desired

Stir together first 4 ingredients and tequila, if desired. Sprinkle each serving with cinnamon, if desired.

Makes 8 cups

Prep Time: 8 minutes

Coconut Rice Pudding

2 cups water
1 cup uncooked long-grain rice
1 tablespoon unsalted butter
Pinch salt
18 ounces evaporated milk
1 can (14 ounces) cream of coconut
½ cup golden raisins
3 egg yolks, beaten
Peel of 2 limes
1 teaspoon vanilla extract

SLOW COOKER DIRECTIONS

1. In a medium saucepan, bring water, rice, butter and salt to a rolling boil, stirring frequently. Reduce heat to a simmer. Cover and cook 10 to 12 minutes. Remove from heat. Set aside, covered, 5 minutes.

2. Meanwhile, spray slow cooker with nonstick cooking spray or lightly grease. Add milk, cream of coconut, raisins, egg yolks, lime peel and vanilla extract; mix well. Add rice mixture; stir to combine. Cover and cook on HIGH 2 hours or on LOW 4 hours. Stir every 30 minutes, if possible. Pudding will thicken as it cools. *Makes 6 (¾ cup) servings*

Mango Coconut Tropical Freeze

1 jar (26 ounces) refrigerated mango slices, drained (or the flesh of 3 ripe mangoes, peeled and cut to equal about 3⅓ cups)
½ cup canned coconut cream
1 tablespoon lime juice
⅓ cup toasted chopped pecans

1. Place mango, coconut cream and lime juice in food processor; process 1 to 2 minutes or until smooth.

2. Spoon into small dessert cups or custard cups. Top with pecans. Place cups on pie plate, cover tightly. Freeze 8 hours or overnight. Remove from freezer and allow to thaw slightly before serving. Serve immediately. *Makes 4 servings*

Lemon Cheese Quesadillas with Mango Sauce

4 (7-inch) flour tortillas
1 cup part-skim ricotta cheese
1/3 cup nonfat vanilla yogurt
1/4 cup lemon juice, divided
1 1/2 tablespoons sugar
2 teaspoons grated lemon peel
1 teaspoon vanilla
1 ripe large mango
1/2 jalapeño pepper,* seeded and minced (optional)
2 tablespoons lightly packed fresh mint, fresh cilantro or fresh basil, plus 4 sprigs for garnish
1 firm ripe banana, cut into 1/4-inch-thick rounds
1/2 pint fresh strawberries, quartered

*Jalapeño peppers can sting and irritate the skin; wear rubber gloves when handling peppers and do not touch eyes. Wash hands after handling peppers.

1. Preheat oven to 375°F.

2. Place tortillas on center oven rack. Bake 6 to 7 minutes or until golden. Place on plate.

3. Combine ricotta, yogurt, 1 tablespoon lemon juice, sugar, lemon peel and vanilla in small bowl. Spread about 1/3 cup over each tortilla.

4. Peel mango. Cut fruit away from pit; chop fruit into 1/2-inch cubes. Place half of mango in food processor or blender. Add 2 tablespoons lemon juice, jalapeño pepper, if desired, and mint; process until puréed.

5. Place remaining mango cubes in small bowl with banana, strawberries and remaining 1 tablespoon lemon juice; toss gently to combine. Spoon 1/2 cup fruit on each tortilla. Drizzle with about 1 tablespoon sauce. Garnish with mint sprigs. *Makes 4 servings*

Lemon Cheese Quesadilla
with Mango Sauce

Mexican Sugar Cookies (Polvorones)

1 cup butter, softened
½ cup powdered sugar
2 tablespoons milk
1 teaspoon vanilla
1 teaspoon ground cinnamon, divided
1½ to 1¾ cups all-purpose flour
1 teaspoon baking powder
1 cup granulated sugar
1 square (1 ounce) semisweet chocolate, finely grated

1. Preheat oven to 325°F. Grease cookie sheets; set aside.

2. Beat butter, powdered sugar, milk, vanilla and ½ teaspoon cinnamon in large bowl with electric mixer at medium speed until light and fluffy, scraping down side of bowl once. Gradually add 1½ cups flour and baking powder. Beat at low speed until well blended, scraping down side of bowl once. Stir in additional flour with spoon if dough is too soft to shape.

3. Roll tablespoonfuls of dough into 1¼-inch balls. Place balls 3 inches apart on prepared cookie sheets. Flatten each ball into 2-inch round with bottom of glass dipped in granulated sugar.

4. Bake 20 to 25 minutes or until edges are golden brown. Let stand on cookie sheets 3 to 4 minutes.

5. Meanwhile, combine granulated sugar, grated chocolate and remaining ½ teaspoon cinnamon in small bowl; stir to combine. Transfer cookies, one at a time, with spatula to sugar mixture; coat on both sides. Remove with spatula to wire racks; cool completely.

6. Store tightly covered at room temperature or freeze up to 3 months.

Makes about 2 dozen cookies

Mexican Sugar Cookies (Polvorones)

Date Menenas

2¾ cups all-purpose flour
½ teaspoon baking powder
¾ cup sugar
⅔ cup FLEISCHMANN'S® Original Spread, softened
1 teaspoon vanilla extract
¼ cup EGG BEATERS® Healthy Real Egg Product
8 ounces pitted dates, finely chopped
½ cup water
1 tablespoon lemon juice

In medium bowl, combine flour and baking powder. Reserve 2 tablespoons sugar for date filling. In large bowl of electric mixer, on medium speed, beat margarine and remaining sugar until creamy. On low speed, add vanilla and egg product alternately with flour mixture. Beat until well combined. Form into flattened disk and wrap in plastic wrap. Refrigerate 1 hour.

To make date filling, place dates, water, reserved sugar and lemon juice in medium saucepan. Bring to a simmer; reduce heat and simmer, covered, 10 minutes. Remove from heat and let cool to room temperature.

Preheat oven to 400°F. Cut dough in half. On floured waxed paper, roll dough to 12×10-inch rectangle. Spread half the filling (½ cup) on dough. Beginning with 12-inch side, roll up as a jelly-roll. With thread, cut ⅜-inch cookies from log. Place on greased cookie sheet. Repeat with remaining dough and filling.

Bake 10 minutes or until bottoms are lightly browned. Remove to wire rack to cool. Store in airtight container.   *Makes about 5 dozen cookies*

Fruit 'n Spice Margarita

    1 cup boiling water
    3 bags LIPTON® SOOTHING MOMENTS® Regular or Decaffeinated Orange & Spice Tea Bags
    ⅓ cup sugar
    1 cup frozen strawberries
    ¼ cup tequila (optional)
    1½ tablespoons lemon juice
    1 cup ice cubes (about 6 to 8)

In teapot, pour boiling water over orange & spice tea bags; cover and steep 5 minutes. Remove tea bags. Stir in sugar and chill.

In blender, process chilled tea mixture, strawberries, tequila, if desired, and lemon juice until blended. Add ice cubes, one at a time, and process at high speed until blended.   *Makes about 2 servings*

Variation: Use 3 LIPTON® Raspberry or Blackberry Tea Bags.

Microwave Directions: Substitute 1 cup cold water for boiling water. In 1-cup glass measure, combine water with orange & spice tea bags. Microwave at HIGH (Full Power) 2 minutes or until very hot. (Tea should not boil.) Let stand 5 minutes. Remove tea bags; stir in sugar and chill. Proceed as directed.

Lacy Tortilla Hearts

    4 (8-inch) flour tortillas
    3 tablespoons butter or margarine, melted
    2 tablespoons vegetable oil
      Powdered sugar

1. Cut out ¾- to 1-inch heart shapes evenly throughout tortillas; discard hearts. Place tortillas in 15×10×1-inch jelly-roll pan.

2. Combine butter and oil in small bowl; pour evenly over tortillas. Let stand 15 minutes.

3. Preheat oven to 400°F.

4. Place tortillas in single layer in additional jelly-roll pans or on rimmed baking sheets. Bake 7 to 10 minutes or until crisp. Place tortillas on wire racks or waxed-paper-covered baking sheets. Cool completely. Sprinkle generously with powdered sugar.   *Makes 4 servings*

Variation: Omit powdered sugar. Combine 1 tablespoon red colored sugar with ⅛ teaspoon cinnamon; mix well. Sprinkle over warm tortillas.

Southwest Baked Apples with Almond Cream

4 medium Braeburn or golden delicious apples, cored within ½ inch of base
½ teaspoon pumpkin pie spice
5 teaspoons butter
5 teaspoons dark brown sugar
3 tablespoons granulated sugar
⅛ teaspoon ground cinnamon
1 cup whipping cream
1 teaspoon almond extract

1. Arrange apples in microwavable 8-inch glass pie plate, leaving 1 inch between apples. Sprinkle pumpkin pie spice into and over each apple. Place 1 teaspoon butter in center of each apple. Place remaining 1 teaspoon butter in center of plate. Place 1 teaspoon brown sugar in center of each apple. Sprinkle remaining 1 teaspoon in center of plate.

2. Microwave apples at HIGH 10 to 12 minutes or until tender. Turn each apple after 3 to 5 minutes. (Cooking time will vary depending on type and exact size of apple; check for tenderness when turning apples and adjust time accordingly.) Remove plate. Spoon carmelized butter and brown sugar from plate bottom over apples. Set aside.

3. Mix granulated sugar and cinnamon in small bowl. Set aside. Beat whipping cream in medium bowl with electric mixer until foamy. With mixer running, slowly add sugar mixture; beat until thickened. Add almond extract; beat until soft peaks form.

4. Place apples on individual serving plates; top with Almond Cream.   *Makes 4 servings*

Serving Suggestion: Serve with after-dinner coffee spiked with coffee liqueur and a cinnamon stick stirrer.

Prep and Cook Time: 20 minutes

Southwest Baked Apple
with Almond Cream

Fire and Ice

2 cups vanilla ice milk or low-fat ice cream
2 teaspoons finely chopped jalapeño pepper*
1 teaspoon grated lime peel, divided
1 cup water
¼ cup sugar
1 cup peeled and chopped kiwifruit
1 tablespoon lime juice
1 cup fresh raspberries

*Jalapeño peppers can sting and irritate the skin; wear rubber gloves when handling peppers and do not touch eyes. Wash hands after handling peppers.

1. Soften ice milk slightly in small bowl. Stir in jalapeño pepper and ½ teaspoon lime peel. Freeze until firm.

2. Combine water, sugar and remaining ½ teaspoon lime peel in small saucepan; bring to a boil. Boil, uncovered, 5 minutes or until reduced by about one-third. Remove from heat and cool to room temperature.

3. Place kiwifruit and lime juice in blender or food processor; process until blended. Stir in water mixture. Pour through fine strainer to remove kiwifruit seeds and lime peel, pressing liquid through strainer with back of spoon. Refrigerate kiwifruit mixture until cold.

4. Pour ¼ cup kiwifruit mixture into each of 6 chilled bowls. Scoop ⅓ cup jalapeño ice milk in center of each bowl. Sprinkle raspberries evenly on top. Garnish with lime peel strips, if desired.

Makes 6 servings

Chocolate-Rum Parfaits

6 to 6½ ounces Mexican chocolate, coarsely chopped*
1½ cups heavy or whipping cream, divided
3 tablespoons golden rum (optional)
¾ teaspoon vanilla extract
Additional whipped cream, for garnish
Sliced almonds, for garnish
Cookies (optional)

*Or, substitute 6 ounces semi-sweet chocolate, coarsely chopped, 1 tablespoon ground cinnamon and ¼ teaspoon almond extract for Mexican chocolate.

Combine chocolate and 3 tablespoons cream in top of double boiler. Heat over simmering water until smooth, stirring occasionally. Gradually stir in rum, if desired; remove top pan from heat. Let stand at room temperature 15 minutes to cool slightly.

Combine remaining cream and vanilla in chilled small bowl. Beat with electric mixer at low speed, then gradually increase speed until stiff but not dry peaks form.

Gently fold whipped cream into cooled chocolate mixture until uniform in color. Spoon mousse into 4 individual dessert dishes. Refrigerate 2 to 3 hours until firm. Garnish with additional whipped cream and sliced almonds. Serve with cookies, if desired. *Makes 4 servings*

Chocolate-Rum Parfaits

Honey Sopaipillas

¼ cup plus 2 teaspoons sugar, divided
½ teaspoon ground cinnamon
2 cups all-purpose flour
½ teaspoon salt
2 teaspoons baking powder
2 tablespoons shortening
¾ cup warm water
  Vegetable oil for deep-frying
  Honey

Combine ¼ cup sugar and cinnamon in small bowl; set aside. Combine remaining 2 teaspoons sugar, flour, salt and baking powder. Add shortening. With fingers, pastry blender or 2 knives, rub or cut in shortening until mixture resembles fine crumbs. Gradually add water; stir with fork until mixture forms dough. Turn out onto lightly floured board; knead 2 minutes or until smooth. Shape into a ball; cover with bowl and let rest 30 minutes.

Divide dough into 4 equal portions; shape each into a ball. Flatten each ball to form circle about 8 inches in diameter and ⅛ inch thick. Cut each round into 4 wedges.

Pour oil into electric skillet or deep heavy pan to depth of 1½ inches. Heat to 360°F. Cook dough, 2 pieces at a time, 2 minutes or until puffed and golden brown, turning once during cooking. Remove from oil with slotted spoon; drain on paper towels. Sprinkle with cinnamon-sugar mixture. Repeat with remaining sopaipillas. Serve hot with honey.   *Makes 16 sopaipillas*

Señor Says: **These delicious sopaipillas can also be served with syrup that has been flavored with anise or cinnamon.**

Creamy Caramel Flan

¾ **cup sugar**

4 **eggs**

1¾ **cups water**

1 **(14-ounce) can EAGLE® BRAND Sweetened Condensed Milk (NOT evaporated milk)**

1 **teaspoon vanilla extract**

⅛ **teaspoon salt**

Sugar Garnish (recipe follows), if desired

1. Preheat oven to 350°F. In heavy skillet over medium heat, cook and stir sugar until melted and caramel-colored. Carefully pour into 8 ungreased 6-ounce custard cups, tilting to coat bottoms.

2. In large mixing bowl, beat eggs; stir in water, Eagle Brand, vanilla and salt. Pour into prepared custard cups. Set cups in large shallow pan. Fill pan with 1 inch hot water.

3. Bake 25 minutes or until knife inserted near centers comes out clean. Cool. Chill. To serve, invert flans onto individual serving plates. Top with Sugar Garnish, if desired, or garnish as desired. Store covered in refrigerator.
Makes 8 servings

Margaritas, Albuquerque Style

1 **lime, cut into wedges**

Coarse salt

1 **can (6 ounces) frozen lime concentrate**

¾ **cup tequila**

6 **tablespoons Triple Sec**

1 **can (12 ounces) lemon-lime or grapefruit soda**

3 **to 4 cups ice cubes**

Lime twist for garnish

Lime peel for garnish

Rub rim of each cocktail glass with lime wedge; swirl glass in salt to coat rim. Combine half of each of the remaining ingredients, except garnishes, in blender container; blend until ice is finely chopped and mixture is slushy. Pour into salt-rimmed glasses. Repeat with remaining ingredients. Garnish, if desired.
Makes 7 to 8 servings

Mango-Orange Mousse

1 large can (28 ounces) mangoes *or* **2 small cans (15 ounces each) mangoes, drained**
1 envelope (1 tablespoon) unflavored gelatin
¼ cup cold water
3 eggs (room temperature), separated
¾ cup orange juice
½ cup sugar, divided
1 tablespoon lemon juice
Dash salt
2 tablespoons rum
1 cup heavy cream, divided
Shredded orange peel for garnish
Mint sprig for garnish

Process enough of the mangoes in blender or food processor container fitted with metal blade to make 1 cup purée. Thinly slice remaining mangoes; cover. Refrigerate; reserve for garnish.

Sprinkle gelatin over cold water in small bowl; let stand 1 minute to soften. Beat egg yolks with whisk in heavy 1-quart pan. Whisk in orange juice, ¼ cup sugar, lemon juice and salt. Cook over medium-low heat, stirring constantly, until mixture has thickened enough to lightly coat metal spoon. Remove from heat; add softened gelatin and stir until dissolved. Stir in mango purée and rum. Refrigerate (or stir over ice water) until mixture mounds slightly when dropped from spoon.

Beat egg whites in large bowl of electric mixer on high speed until frothy. Gradually add remaining ¼ cup sugar, 1 tablespoon at a time, beating well after each addition. Beat until stiff peaks form; fold into mango mixture. Without washing bowl or beaters, whip ½ cup of the cream until soft peaks form. Fold into mango mixture. Spoon into glass serving bowl. Refrigerate until firm, 3 to 4 hours or up to 24 hours. Just before serving, whip remaining ½ cup cream until soft peaks form. Garnish mousse with reserved mango slices, whipped cream, orange peel and mint. *Makes 6 to 8 servings*

Mango-Orange Mousse

New Mexican Hot Chocolate

¼ cup unsweetened cocoa powder
¼ cup sugar
½ teaspoon ground cinnamon
¼ teaspoon ground nutmeg
   Dash salt
⅔ cup water
3⅓ cups milk
1 teaspoon vanilla extract
4 cinnamon sticks

Combine cocoa, sugar, ground cinnamon, nutmeg, salt and water in 3-quart saucepan. Cook, stirring occasionally, over medium heat until cocoa and sugar are dissolved. Add milk and vanilla. Heat to simmering. Whip mixture with rotary beater or portable electric mixer until frothy. Pour into four mugs. Place one cinnamon stick in each mug.   *Makes 4 servings*

Berry Berry Mockarita

½ cup boiling water
1 LIPTON® Brisk Cup Size Regular or Decaffeinated Tea Bag
2 tablespoons sugar
½ cup strawberries
3 tablespoons chilled orange juice
1 tablespoon lime juice
   Dash ground cinnamon
½ cup ice cubes (about 3 to 4)

1. In teapot, pour boiling water over tea bag; cover and brew 5 minutes. Remove tea bag; stir in sugar and cool.

2. In blender, process tea with remaining ingredients except ice cubes until blended. Add ice cubes, one at a time, and process at high speed until blended. Serve, if desired, in stemmed glass with sugar-coated rim. Garnish, if desired, with fresh strawberries or orange slice.   *Makes 1 serving*

Top to bottom: New Mexican Hot Chocolate and Biscochitos (page 358)

Banana-Rum Custard with Vanilla Wafers

1½ cups milk

3 eggs

½ cup sugar

3 tablespoons dark rum or milk

⅛ teaspoon salt

1 medium banana, sliced ¼ inch thick

15 to 18 vanilla wafers

Sliced strawberries, raspberries or kiwis for garnish (optional)

SLOW COOKER DIRECTIONS

1. Beat milk, eggs, sugar, rum and salt in medium bowl. Pour into 1-quart casserole. Do not cover.

2. Add rack to 5-quart slow cooker and pour in 1 cup water. Place casserole on rack. Cover and cook on LOW 3½ to 4 hours. Remove casserole from slow cooker. Arrange banana slices and wafers over custard. Garnish with strawberries, raspberries or kiwis, if desired.   *Makes 5 servings*

Banana-Rum Custard with Vanilla Wafers

Biscochitos

3 cups all-purpose flour
2 teaspoons anise seeds
1½ teaspoons baking powder
½ teaspoon salt
1 cup butter
¾ cup sugar, divided
1 egg
¼ cup orange juice
2 teaspoons ground cinnamon

Preheat oven to 350°F. Combine flour, anise seeds, baking powder and salt in medium bowl; set aside. Beat butter in large bowl with electric mixer at medium speed until creamy. Add ½ cup sugar; beat until fluffy. Blend in egg. Gradually add flour mixture alternately with orange juice, mixing well after each addition.

Divide dough in half. Roll out one portion at a time on lightly floured surface to ¼-inch thickness; cover remaining dough to prevent drying. Cut out cookies with fancy cookie cutters 2 to 2½ inches in diameter, adding scraps to remaining dough. If dough becomes too soft to handle, refrigerate briefly. Place cookies 1 inch apart on ungreased baking sheets.

Combine remaining ¼ cup sugar and cinnamon; lightly sprinkle over cookies. Bake 8 to 10 minutes or until edges are lightly browned. Let cool on wire racks; store in airtight container.

Makes 4 to 5 dozen cookies

Mexican Chocolate Macaroons

1 package (8 ounces) semisweet baking chocolate, divided
1¾ cups plus ⅓ cup whole almonds, divided
¾ cup sugar
1 teaspoon ground cinnamon
1 teaspoon vanilla
2 egg whites

1. Preheat oven to 400°F. Grease baking sheets; set aside.

2. Place 5 squares chocolate in food processor; process until coarsely chopped. Add 1¾ cups almonds and sugar; process using on/off pulsing action until mixture is finely ground. Add cinnamon, vanilla and egg whites; process just until mixture forms moist dough.

3. Form dough into 1-inch balls (dough will be sticky). Place about 2 inches apart on prepared baking sheets. Press 1 almond on top of each cookie.

4. Bake 8 to 10 minutes or just until set. Cool 2 minutes on baking sheets. Remove cookies from baking sheets to wire racks. Cool completely.

5. Heat remaining 3 squares chocolate in small saucepan over very low heat until melted. Spoon chocolate into small resealable plastic food storage bag. Cut small corner off bottom of bag with scissors. Drizzle chocolate over cookies.   *Makes 3 dozen cookies*

Tip: For longer storage, allow cookies to stand until chocolate drizzle is set. Store in airtight containers.

Prep and Bake Time: 30 minutes

Rice Pudding Mexicana

1 package instant rice pudding
1 tablespoon vanilla
¼ teaspoon ground cinnamon
  Dash ground cloves
¼ cup slivered almonds
  Additional ground cinnamon

1. Prepare rice pudding according to package directions.

2. Remove pudding from heat; stir in vanilla, ¼ teaspoon cinnamon and cloves. Pour into individual dessert dishes.

3. Sprinkle with almonds and additional cinnamon. Serve warm.   *Makes 6 servings*

Prep and Cook Time: 18 minutes

Tex-Mex Brownies

½ cup butter
2 squares (1 ounce each) unsweetened chocolate
½ to 1 teaspoon ground red pepper
2 eggs
1 cup sugar
½ cup all-purpose flour
1 teaspoon vanilla
1 cup (6 ounces) semisweet chocolate chips

Preheat oven to 325°F. Grease and flour an 8-inch square pan. Melt butter and unsweetened chocolate in small heavy saucepan over low heat. Remove from heat. Stir in pepper; cool. Beat eggs in medium bowl until light. Add sugar, beating well. Blend in chocolate mixture. Stir in flour and vanilla. Spread batter evenly in prepared pan. Bake 30 minutes or until firm in center. Remove from oven; sprinkle chocolate chips over the top. Let stand until chocolate is melted, then spread evenly over brownies. Cool completely in pan on wire rack. Cut into 2-inch squares.   *Makes 16 brownies*

Rice Pudding Mexicana

Mexican Wedding Cookies

1 cup pecan pieces or halves
1 cup butter, softened
2 cups powdered sugar, divided
2 cups all-purpose flour, divided
2 teaspoons vanilla
⅛ teaspoon salt

1. Place pecans in food processor. Process using on/off pulsing action until pecans are ground, but not pasty.

2. Beat butter and ½ cup powdered sugar in large bowl with electric mixer at medium speed until light and fluffy. Gradually add 1 cup flour, vanilla and salt. Beat at low speed until well blended. Stir in remaining 1 cup flour and ground nuts with spoon. Shape dough into ball; wrap in plastic wrap and refrigerate 1 hour or until firm.

3. Preheat oven to 350°F. Shape tablespoons of dough into 1-inch balls. Place 1 inch apart on ungreased cookie sheets.

4. Bake 12 to 15 minutes or until pale golden brown. Let cookies stand on cookie sheets 2 minutes.

5. Meanwhile, place 1 cup powdered sugar in 13×9-inch glass dish. Transfer hot cookies to powdered sugar. Roll cookies in powdered sugar, coating well. Let cookies cool in sugar.

6. Sift remaining ½ cup powdered sugar over sugar-coated cookies before serving. Store tightly covered at room temperature or freeze up to 1 month.   *Makes about 4 dozen cookies*

Mexican Wedding Cookies

Flan

2 cups sugar, divided
½ cup water
1 package (8 ounces) PHILADELPHIA® Cream Cheese, softened
1 can (13 ounces) evaporated milk
4 eggs
1 teaspoon vanilla
　 Dash salt

MIX 1 cup of the sugar and water in heavy saucepan. Bring to boil over medium-high heat. Boil until syrup turns deep golden brown. Remove from heat; immediately pour into 8- or 9-inch round cake pan, tilting pan to distribute syrup evenly on bottom.

BEAT cream cheese and remaining 1 cup sugar with electric mixer on medium speed until well blended. Gradually add milk, beating well after each addition. Blend in eggs, vanilla and salt. Pour into prepared pan.

PLACE pan in large baking pan; place in oven. Pour boiling water into larger pan to come about ¾ of the way up side of cake pan.

BAKE at 350°F for 1 hour and 20 minutes or until knife inserted near center comes out clean. Remove cake pan from water; cool. Cover. Refrigerate several hours. To serve, run metal spatula around edge of pan. Unmold onto serving plate. *Makes 8 to 10 servings*

Prep: 30 minutes plus refrigerating
Bake: 1 hour 20 minutes

Flan

Basics

Flour Tortillas

    2 cups all-purpose flour
    ½ teaspoon salt
    ¼ cup vegetable shortening
    ½ cup warm water

1. Combine flour and salt in medium bowl. Rub shortening into flour with fingertips until mixture has fine, even texture. Stir in water until dough forms.

2. Knead dough on floured surface 2 to 3 minutes until smooth and elastic. Wrap in plastic wrap. Let stand 30 minutes at room temperature.

3. Knead dough a few times. Divide evenly into 8 pieces for 10-inch tortillas or 12 pieces for 8-inch tortillas. Shape pieces into balls; cover with plastic wrap to prevent them from drying out.

4. Using rolling pin, roll out each dough ball on floured surface, turning over frequently, into 8- or 10-inch circle. Stack each tortilla between sheets of waxed paper.

5. Heat ungreased heavy griddle or skillet over medium-high heat until a little water sprinkled on surface sizzles. Carefully lay 1 tortilla on griddle; cook 20 or 30 seconds until top is bubbly and bottom is flecked with brown spots. Turn tortilla over; cook 15 to 20 seconds until flecked with brown spots. If tortilla puffs up while second side is cooking, press it down gently with spatula. Remove tortilla to foil.

6. Cook remaining tortillas as directed in step 5. If griddle becomes too hot, reduce heat to prevent burning. Stack cooked tortillas and cover with foil until all are cooked. Use immediately or wrap in foil and keep warm in 250°F oven up to 30 minutes. Tortillas are best when fresh, but can be wrapped in foil and refrigerated up to 3 days or frozen up to 2 weeks. Reheat in 350°F oven 10 minutes before using.   *Makes 8 (10-inch) or 12 (8-inch) tortillas*

Corn Tortillas

2 cups masa harina
1 to 1¼ cups warm water

1. Cut 2 (7-inch) squares from heavy-duty plastic bag. Combine masa harina and 1 cup water in medium bowl. Add remaining water, 1 tablespoon at a time, until a smooth stiff dough is formed.

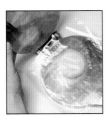

2. Test consistency of dough by rolling 1 piece dough into 1¾-inch ball; flatten slightly. Place ball on piece of plastic on lower plate of tortilla press, slightly off-center away from handle.* Cover with second piece of plastic; press down firmly with top of press to make 6-inch tortilla. Peel off top piece of plastic; invert tortilla onto hand and peel off second piece of plastic. If edges are cracked or ragged, dough is too dry; mix in water, 1 to 2 teaspoons at a time, until dough presses out with smooth edges. If tortilla sticks to plastic, dough is too wet; mix in masa harina, 1 tablespoon at a time, until dough no longer sticks when pressed.

3. When dough has correct consistency, divide evenly into 12 pieces for 6-inch tortillas or 24 pieces for 4-inch tortillas. Shape pieces into balls; cover with plastic wrap to prevent them from drying out.

4. Press out tortillas as directed in step 2, stacking between sheets of plastic wrap or waxed paper.

5. Heat ungreased heavy griddle or skillet over medium-high heat until a little water sprinkled on surface dances. Carefully lay 1 tortilla on griddle; cook 30 seconds or until edges begin to dry out. Turn tortilla over; cook 45 seconds to 1 minute until dry and lightly flecked with brown spots. Turn tortilla over again; cook first side 15 to 20 seconds more until dry and light brown. During last stage of cooking, tortilla may puff up; do not press down. Remove tortilla to kitchen towel; it will be slightly stiff, but will soften as it stands.

6. Cook remaining tortillas as directed in step 5. If griddle becomes too hot, reduce heat to prevent burning. Stack cooked tortillas and keep wrapped in towel until all are cooked. Use immediately or wrap in foil and keep warm in 250°F oven up to 30 minutes. Tortillas are best when fresh, but can be wrapped in foil and refrigerated up to 3 days or frozen up to 2 weeks. Reheat in 350°F oven 10 minutes before using.
Makes 12 (6-inch) or 24 (4-inch) tortillas

*A tortilla press works best, but if necessary, you can press with bottom of pie plate or heavy skillet.

Guacamole

2 large avocados, pitted and peeled
¼ cup finely chopped tomato
2 tablespoons lime juice or lemon juice
2 tablespoons grated onion with juice
½ teaspoon salt
¼ teaspoon hot pepper sauce
   Black pepper to taste
   Additional chopped tomato (optional)

Place avocados in medium bowl; mash coarsely with fork. Stir in tomato, lime juice, onion with juice, salt and pepper sauce; mix well. Add black pepper. Spoon into serving container. Serve immediately or cover and refrigerate up to 2 hours. Garnish with additional chopped tomato, if desired.   *Makes 2 cups*

Tip: To quickly ripen hard avocados, store them in a loosely closed paper bag at room temperature.

Classic Salsa

4 medium tomatoes
1 small onion, finely chopped
2 to 3 jalapeño peppers or serrano peppers,* seeded and minced
¼ cup chopped fresh cilantro
1 small clove garlic, minced
2 tablespoons lime juice
   Salt and black pepper to taste

*Jalapeño and serrano peppers can sting and irritate the skin; wear rubber gloves when handling peppers and do not touch eyes. Wash hands after handling.

Cut tomatoes in half; remove seeds. Coarsely chop tomatoes. Combine tomatoes, onion, jalapeño peppers, cilantro, garlic and lime juice in medium bowl. Add salt and black pepper. Cover and refrigerate 1 hour or up to 3 days for flavors to blend.   *Makes about 2½ cups*

Refried Beans

8 ounces dried red, pink or pinto beans (1⅓ cups)
4½ cups cold water
⅓ cup plus 1 tablespoon vegetable shortening or vegetable oil, divided
1 small white onion, sliced
1½ teaspoons salt
1 small white onion, finely chopped
1 small clove garlic, minced

1. Rinse beans thoroughly in sieve under cold running water, picking out any debris or blemished beans.

2. Place beans, water, 1 tablespoon shortening and sliced onion in 3-quart saucepan. Bring to a boil over high heat. Reduce heat to low. Cover and simmer 1½ hours or just until beans are tender, not soft.

3. Stir in salt. Cover and simmer over very low heat 30 to 45 minutes until beans are very soft. Do not drain.*

4. Heat remaining ⅓ cup shortening in heavy, large skillet over high heat until very hot. Add chopped onion and garlic. Reduce heat to medium. Cook and stir 4 minutes or until onion is softened.

*Flavor is improved if beans are prepared to this point, then refrigerated, covered, overnight before completing recipe.

5. Increase heat to high. Add 1 cup undrained beans. Cook and stir, mashing beans with bean or potato masher.

6. As beans begin to dry, add another 1 cup undrained beans. Cook and stir, mashing beans with bean or potato masher. Repeat until all beans and cooking liquid have been added and mixture is a coarse purée. Adjust heat as needed to prevent beans from sticking and burning. Total cooking time will be around 20 minutes.

7. Beans may be served as a side dish or used as an ingredient for another recipe.

Makes about 2 cups

Acknowledgments

The publisher would like to thank the companies and organizations listed below for the use of their recipes and photographs in this publication.

A.1.® Steak Sauce

American Lamb Council

Birds Eye®

Bob Evans®

ConAgra Foods®

Del Monte Corporation

Eagle® Brand

Egg Beaters®

The Golden Grain Company®

Grandma's® is a registered trademark of Mott's, Inc.

Guiltless Gourmet®

Hebrew National®

Heinz U.S.A.

The Hidden Valley® Food Products Company

Hormel Foods, LLC

Kellogg Company

The Kingsford Products Company

Kraft Foods Holdings

Lawry's® Foods, Inc.

McIlhenny Company (TABASCO® brand Pepper Sauce)

Minnesota Cultivated Wild Rice Council

National Fisheries Institute

National Onion Association

National Pork Board

National Turkey Federation

Nestlé USA

Newman's Own, Inc.®

North Dakota Beef Commission

Perdue Farms Incorporated

Reckitt Benckiser

Riviana Foods Inc.

Sargento® Foods Inc.

The J.M. Smucker Company

Uncle Ben's Inc.

Unilever Bestfoods North America

USA Rice Federation

Wisconsin Milk Marketing Board

Index